JIG FISHING FOR STEELHEAD & SALMON

DAVE VEDDER

JIG FISHING FOR STEELHEAD & SALMON

DAVE VEDDER

Frank Amato
PORTLAND

DEDICATION

My wife, Pam, has been my confidant, editor, occasional critic and always my best friend. For more than 35 years she has tended the home fires while I cover the globe, always in search of another fishing fix. Every article and book I have written, she has edited. Even though she seldom fishes, Pam knows more about the subject than many serious anglers do. Few wives would have put up with my frequent fishing adventures, the egg cure stains on the Formica, the smelly fishing vests and my inability to cross any river without gawking to see how the water is looking today. Whatever degree of success I have attained is primarily due to her patience, good nature and generous spirit. Pam, this is for you!

Frank Amato Publications, Inc, P.O. Box 82112, Portland, Oregon 97282

503.653.8108 • www.amatobooks.com

Photographs by the author unless otherwise noted.

Jig photos by Jim Schollmeyer

Book & Cover Design: Kathy Johnson

Printed in Singapore

Softbound ISBN-13: 978-1-57188-391-9 UPC: 0-81127-00225-2

3 5 7 9 10 8 6 4 2

CONTENTS

INTRODUCTION

"WHY ANOTHER JIG-FISHING BOOK?" several friends have asked. The answer is simple. We steelhead and salmon anglers have learned so much since the publication of my first jig-fishing book, that a new book is demanded to cover new techniques, new jigs and jig-making materials, how to make jigs and especially how to catch more salmon using jigs. When I wrote my first book on jig-fishing, I understood there were other anglers who knew many tricks and techniques I had not been exposed to. Naturally, I talked to the best jig fishers I could find, and their assistance was invaluable. Nevertheless, today, in part because of that first book, jig-fishing for steelhead and salmon is exponentially more popular than it was ten years ago. As a result, the thousands of anglers who now consider jigs their go-to lure have learned countless new tricks for 'taking steelhead and salmon. In recent years we have learned that jigs are great lures for salmon fishing.

As with my previous book on jig-fishing, I have relied heavily on innovative anglers who have taken the time to try to perfect new techniques, to experiment with new color combinations, to use new materials, and to test new presentations. There are too many great anglers who contributed to this book to list, but I do want to give a special thank you to Nick Amato, Bill Herzog, Dave Kilheffner, John Koenig and Brian Morse for all their help and constant willingness to go out to the river to test our theories.

This is a "how to" book. As such, I have tried to provide all the information you will need to use jigs to dramatically increase your success with steelhead and salmon. In addition, I wanted to give you a bit of history on jig-fishing and try to entertain you with anecdotes that will get your juices flowing and help illustrate important lessons for jig-fishing. In my previous book I spent a good deal of time trying to convince readers that jigs can be effective tools for the serious steelhead and salmon angler. Today, I feel no such need. Almost all serious anglers know that jigs are a major part of the river fisher's arsenal, and most of you know that in many circumstances nothing will outfish a jig. Rather than trying to convince those who need no convincing, I will strive to give you every possible bit of information to make you understand why jigs work so well, how to fish jigs, and where and when jigs work best.

Like many other steelheaders, I was slow to give jigs a try. I had found my share of success with plastic baits, such as Gooey Bobs, Jensen Eggs and pink worms. When those failed me, I would grudgingly switch to natural baits such as sand shrimp, salmon eggs or prawns. When fishing with friends who owned boats, I would try pulling plugs—a steelheading method that I found as boring as it is effective. I saw no reason to find another pocket in my vest for these strange-looking lead-head jigs some people claimed to use with great success. Then some of the best steelheaders I know began telling me about their phenomenal successes with jigs.

The author, 10 years old, in La Push, Washington.

Nick Amato was the first to give me an account of how deadly jigs could be when conditions are less than ideal. He called me on a January day when we had been suffering through a long stretch of cold weather. The rivers were dead low, and river temperatures were in the thirties. No one was having much luck on the steelhead scene. Yet, Nick was so excited I had to ask him to slow down as he told me about his amazing success fishing with jigs. He and the late Rich Paradzinski had fished a deep pool on the Sandy River. Twelve other anglers had been working the pool with every possible combination of steelhead gear when Rich and Nick arrived. Rich rigged up with small floats, light line and 1/8-ounce pink jigs. Within three hours they had hooked fourteen steelhead. The other twelve anglers hadn't taken any. I believed Nick's story, but assumed it was a freak accident. I didn't even consider rushing out to buy some jigs.

Then another friend called to tell me about a day of steelheading on the Wilson River. He had hired a top guide who had fruitlessly pulled plugs most of the day without a strike. My friend finally asked the guide if it would be okay to try some jigs. The guide was skeptical, almost hostile, but my friend persevered. By day's end, my friend, who had been casting jigs, while the guide

This is what keeps us awake all night before a trip to our favorite river.

continued to pull plugs, had three steelhead. The plugs hadn't taken any. That story convinced me to buy a few jigs, which I carried, but didn't use, for over a year.

My conversion came on the Wenatchee River on a golden fall day. I had been working a pool that I knew held fish—it always had before, and I had seen two fish roll near the tailout. I literally tossed everything in my vest at them—spinners, spoons, and artificial eggs, even my trusty pink worm. Nothing! Finally, with more hope than expectation, I tied a pink-and-white 1/4-ounce jig beneath a small float. On my second cast the float was yanked under. I set the hook, too hard, and broke off a fine, red-cheek steelhead. With shaking hands I tied on my only other jig, a chartreuse-and-black 1/4-ounce model. Three casts later, I had hooked my second steelhead on a jig. By now, of course, I was hooked as well.

The day that really completed my conversion to jigs came on the Kalum River. We were fishing with an old-time guide, now retired, who had used nothing but spawn bags for years. I spent a good bit of the day extolling the virtues of jigs and could tell he was unimpressed. As luck would have it, on the first day my partner, who must go unnamed for reasons you will soon understand, hooked only one fish on spawn bags while I hooked seven. I felt bad that he had had such a poor day, but didn't know what I could do to make him feel better. The second day I told my friend I was going to use jigs all day and that he should continue to fish spawn bags. My thinking was that surely a nice spawn bag would outfish a jig. I was wrong! By day's end he had two fish and I had eleven. He felt even worse, but I knew that I would never again go steelheading without a selection of jigs in my vest. Moreover, perhaps more importantly, that I would fish those jigs hard, even in preference to bait.

Unfortunately, even after all these years, many anglers haven't learned to use jigs, (I should tell you though, that the friend I fished with on the Kalum that day now uses jigs almost exclusively) and many others who occasionally use jigs are unaware of some tricks and tactics that can increase their success. I bring you this book in the same spirit as the ten-year-old who excitedly calls his friends to tell them how well red worms work for bluegill, or the 70-year-old who shows a new fly to his angling club. I am excited about what I, and the thousands of others who now use jigs, have discovered. In addition, I want to share our find with you. I hope this book will bring you more angling pleasure by increasing your success with river salmon and steelhead.

Ron Fabien grins with joy over a pink salmon taken on a jig in the Snohomish River.

CHAPTER 1

THE HISTORY OF STEELHEADING WITH JIGS

JIGS ARE AMONG THE OLDEST FORM of artificial lures known to man. Depending upon how loosely we define the term "jigs," one can argue that the jig may have been the first artificial lure. If we define a jig as simply a weight and attached attractor, jigs can be traced to the earliest days of sport fishing. There is ample evidence that jigs were very popular in the US as far back as the early 1900s. My revered old copy of *Outdoor Life's Sportsman's Cyclopedia*, circa 1942, advises that jigs are deadly for walleye, trout, bass and many pan fish. They failed to mention steelhead and salmon, perhaps because no one had yet tried tempting steelhead with a jig.

The advent of jig-fishing for steelhead in the Northwest can be traced to a fateful day in 1977 on the Cowlitz River. Steelheading fanatic Leo Gwazacz was having one of those days we all experience now and then—he couldn't buy a strike. In frustration, he began digging through his tackle box to see if he could find something, anything that might prompt a strike. What he found was a small, redheaded, lead jig wrapped with white chenille. He thought it looked like something a steelhead might pick-up, so he tried it. Three casts later, Northwest steelheading was forever changed. A Cowlitz River steelhead proved to Leo what thousands of other steelheaders were eventually to learn; many times, in many places, nothing will outfish a properly presented jig.

At first, Leo wasn't certain whether he had discovered a hot new lure, or if he had just found one kamikaze steelhead. Leo began fishing jigs regularly, and he began taking steelhead regularly. He soon realized that he was onto something big. Leo began making his own jigs, experimenting with various color combinations of chenille body wrap. Eventually, he began sharing his jigs with friends. Within a few years, Leo's success with jigs became well known among Northwest steelhead fanatics. Leo couldn't keep up with demand. He began mass manufacturing and marketing "Leo's Jigs."

In the next few years Leo and his son, Leo Junior, made many changes in the design of their jigs. Leo Junior is credited with the idea of adding colored beads to the hook shank for added attraction. Leo Senior believed the beads remind steelhead of the shape and silhouette of a

shrimp. Whatever the steelhead may think, they certainly go for jigs with bead bodies. Today, Leo's Jigs are still taking steelhead and salmon all across the Northwest.

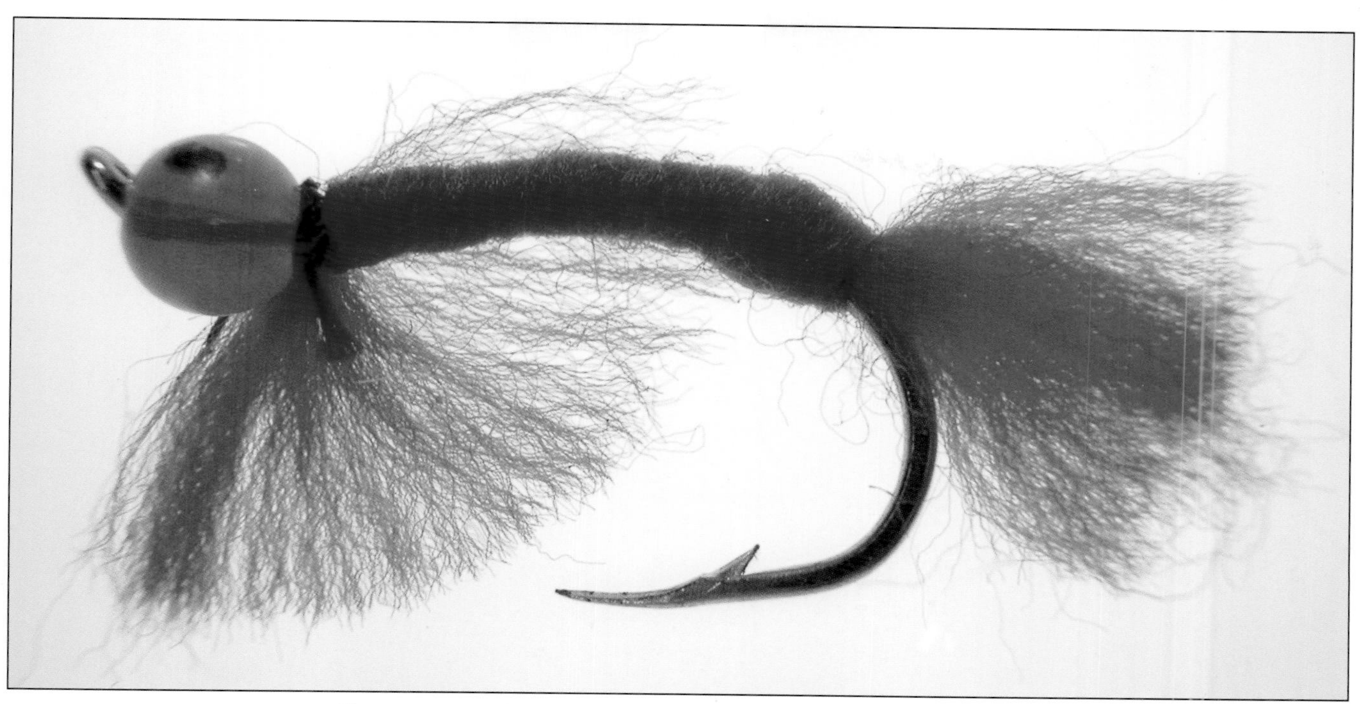

This was one of the innovative lures invented by the late Paul Beaupre.

Paul Beaupre was another pioneer in the Northwest steelhead jig-fishing industry. Paul began manufacturing and selling a line of innovative steelhead and salmon lures in 1982. In the early 1980s one of Paul's favorite lures was the Pearl Head Shrimp, an artificial lure featuring a bead head and a chenille body on a curved hook. It was a dynamite steelhead lure. Paul later noticed that Leo's jigs featured a lead head and a bead body. Paul decided to modify his Pearl Head Shrimp by adding a jig head and beads on the body. The result was the forerunner of the tremendously popular Big Jig and Jig-A-Lou, the latter being named after his wife, Mary Lou.

Great Lakes area steelhead and salmon anglers have long used jigs with deadly results. Many of the region's top anglers use jigs exclusively. The strong preference shown for jigs by Midwest anglers has resulted in a proliferation of jigs of every possible size, shape and color. Great Lakes jig anglers have a choice of more than fifty factory designs and as many homemade varieties as the imagination will allow. Given the huge popularity of jigs in the Great Lakes region, tracing the evolution of jig-fishing to its roots has proven almost impossible. Nevertheless, most Great Lakes anglers agree Gill Rice was one of the pioneers who popularized the use of jigs for steelhead.

Gill's story is much like that of Leo Gwazacz on the west coast, except Gill experienced his revelation at least five years sooner than Leo did. Gill, who was a steelhead guide on the Muskegon River, took a break from steelheading to catch a few yellow perch for dinner. He was using a locally popular perch jig, called a "Tear Drop," in the 1/8-ounce size. Gill fished the small red jig, tipped with a grub. To his surprise, he found he was consistently hooking steelhead on his "perch jig."

Like any serious steelheader, Gill immediately did two things: he kept his discovery a secret and he began tinkering with jigs to find ways to make them more effective. For several years Gill was able to keep his secret. Then one day another angler "accidentally" cast across Gill's line and got a good look at the secret weapon, while untangling the lines. The secret was out. Soon many anglers on the Muskegon and White rivers were steelheading with jigs. Today, many of the region's top rods consider jigs the most deadly possible steelhead

DAVE KILHEFNER

A colorful selection of jigs.

lure. Most Great Lakes anglers combine the visual appeal of jigs with the alluring scent of spawn sacks, grubs or other favorite steelhead baits.

Jig-fishing for steelhead is here to stay in the Northwest and in the Great Lakes. Jig-fishing for salmon is just beginning to catch on, but it, too, will become a standard as more and more anglers learn how deadly a well-presented jig can be. Surprisingly, this effective angling technique has been slow to take hold in British Columbia and Alaska, but successful fishing techniques have a way of spreading rapidly. Soon jigs will be in widespread use wherever steelhead or salmon are found.

The most recent evolution of jig-fishing has been their use for salmon. In the late 80s several Olympic Peninsula guides began experimenting with jigs for coho. In the beginning they used small jig heads coupled with pink plastic hoochies. When properly presented, these jigs are absolutely dynamite for coho. Eventually, the guides' secret leaked out and today many guides and others consider the pink hoochie and jig head a standard for coho.

On rivers in the Puget Sound, anglers now use the pink hoochie in smaller sizes for pink salmon and chum anglers are also rapidly embracing jigs. Chinook anglers have been among the last to switch to jigs, but several Oregon anglers consistently use the jig to good effect. A later chapter will cover the best techniques for targeting salmon with jigs.

Since 1977 countless trophy steelhead have fallen for a well-presented jig.

This Salmon River steelhead was one of the first the author hooked on a jig.

CHAPTER 2

WHY JIGS WORK SO WELL

I BELIEVE THAT PERHAPS THE MOST important reason why jigs work so well for both steelhead and salmon is the simple fact that they sink fast and are in the strike zone almost immediately. This may seem minor to some, but when you consider the number of times we cast each day, a fast-sinking lure that fishes well, almost the instant it hits the water, can give you a huge edge. Another advantage of jigs is the fact that we can buy or make them in any size or color we like, and can use a huge variety of materials to fashion our jigs, ranging from natural products such as schlappen, marabou, and rabbit to synthetics like Flashabou, tinsel and anything else that we believe may appeal to our quarry. In addition, jigs give us a variety of ways to fish them, from the dead drift, usually preferred by steelhead and chums, to the jigging action that coho and pinks love. Few other lures are as versatile as jigs.

Another huge advantage of jigs is the fact that they are most often fished beneath a float. Floats give us the ability to rapidly and accurately adjust to whatever depth we want, the ability to precisely control the line of drift we choose, the ability to instantly detect strikes, and the ability to present the jig in a very natural manner.

Yet, in spite of all the obvious advantages to jigs, there is something almost magical about jigs that I simply cannot explain. Over and over again, I have seen jigs take steelhead when nothing else will get a glance. One afternoon on the Gold River I saw an awesome example of how jigs seem to magically draw a strike when nothing else will. My good friend, Clint Derlago, and I were floating the stretch between the bridges in our pontoon boats. We had never floated that stretch before, so every run we came to presented a new adventure. About three in the afternoon we came to a spot that absolutely screamed steelhead. The head of the run was a narrow gap in bedrock that soon widened to a pebble beach on the left and an undercut rook wall on the right. The river was fishing well. We had landed more than ten steelhead between us already, but this was the finest looking pool we had seen yet.

Clint was not yet a jig convert. He fished the run with spawn bags and with several other rigs that had been working for him. I was new to jig-fishing, but already knew they could be deadly. I fished the run with Clint for more than 20 minutes. Between us we tried six or seven proven steelhead killers. Finally Clint said, “Let’s get out of here. This place looks great, but I don’t think there’s anything here.” I told him that I just knew there had to be fish there. I tied on my favorite jig, a Beau Mac SMJ 2, cerise marabou jig. I cast to the edge of the undercut rock bank and let the jig work along the rock edge. My float hadn’t gone more than 20 feet when it yanked under violently. I set the hook and began battling one of the biggest steelhead I have ever seen in the Gold River. Eventually, we landed a double stripe buck that was 39.5 inches long. We didn’t measure the girth, as we were concerned about stressing the great fish. Once again, the jig had worked its magic.

In more recent years I have seen jigs absolutely slam coho, chum and pink salmon. In fact, for those three

There is something magical about jig-fishing.

Jig-fishing is a great way for beginners and experts alike to catch steelhead. Rob Taylor hoists up one of his first hatchery summer steelhead. It took a red marabou jig fished under a fixed float.

species, I know of no other lure that is as effective. I often fish the Alagnak River in Alaska with my friend Jack Berryman. Jack calls my Flashabou jig "probers," because he knows that if I cast to a likely looking run, the jig will almost always draw a strike if there are any coho present. Jack, a dyed-in-the-wool fly-fisher sometimes gets a bit perturbed when I tie on a jig. He feels that fishing a jig gives me an unfair advantage when he is using a fly. He's right.

WHY STEELHEAD AND SALMON STRIKE A JIG

Steelhead and salmon will pick up or eat a wide variety of objects. I have known and heard of steelhead ingesting fiberglass roofing material, small birds, snakes, and many other strange objects. Salmon in rivers often tend to be closed mouthed, but again, they will pick up or eat many things that we consider strange. I believe that both salmon and steelhead take things in their mouths for one of three reasons: hunger, curiosity and aggression.

HUNGER

For many years the 'experts' have told us that salmon and steelhead never eat anything once they enter fresh water. That is absolute nonsense. Consider the chinook that takes a Kwikfish so deep in its throat that removing the hook is nearly impossible, or the summer-run steelhead that takes a sand shrimp all the way down its throat. I believe steelhead will feed anytime food is available, and the steelhead that have spawned, and are returning back downriver, will eat almost anything that remotely resembles food. Salmon definitely decrease feeding once they enter fresh water, but in the lower reaches of the river they will feed when given the chance. Trolled herring have often proven deadly on chinook as far upriver as the Hanford Reach. Even in the upper stretches of the river some salmon will instinctively take something that reminds them of the food they ate in the river as juveniles or in the ocean as adults.

Jigs can be tied to represent a large variety of naturally occurring food sources, including salmon eggs and shrimp. Yet, I think many salmon and steelhead that take a jig as a food item do so partly out of hunger and partly out of curiosity.

CURIOSITY

Salmon and steelhead are curious creatures. They like to look at strange objects and to touch them. Because they have no hands, fish must pick up objects with their mouths. If you spend any amount of time in an area where hatchery fish are penned or where wild fish are completely undisturbed, you will soon notice that it is not uncommon for them to pick up objects, swim with them a short distance and spit them out. I am convinced that in many cases the fish knew that the object was not a food source, but were simply checking it out the only way it could.

When fishing a jig, many times the take is very subtle. Often, the float will gently lift up, or move ever so slightly sideways or dip down so slightly that you may not be sure whether your eyes are playing tricks on you. Many times these are fish that have picked up the jig and spit it back out after tasting, feeling and generally examining a foreign object in their world. Top jig fishermen are always alert to even the subtlest twitches in their float and set the hook the instant they see any unnatural movement. Often, you can hook a fish that wasn't really striking, but just checking out your jig.

AGGRESSION

Both steelhead and salmon will, on occasion, attack a lure out of aggression. I believe that most strikes on spinners and spoons are aggression strikes. I believe that most takes on jigs are either from curiosity or hunger, as most jigs are not active lures that will trigger an aggressive response like a Kwikfish, spoon or spinner might. However, on occasion a steelhead or salmon will be irritated by a jig and will respond accordingly. I have seen jig takes that were vicious and I'm certain many of these were due to aggression. If a steelhead or salmon believes that the jig is an invader, it will slam it. While aggression will trigger the occasional jig strike, I believe most strikes are the result of either hunger of curiosity. However, when fishing a jig without a float, as we do for coho, pinks and occasionally for steelhead, the takes can be savage. I suspect these are aggression strikes.

SUMMARY

- Jigs are extraordinarily versatile lures.
- Jigs can be made in a huge variety of sizes, colors, and materials.
- Jigs can be fished either under a float or you can swim them without a float.
- Salmon and steelhead take lures in their mouths for three reasons: hunger, curiosity or aggression. Jigs can trigger any of these responses.

MAKING YOUR OWN JIGS

PERHAPS THE GREATEST THRILL YOU can experience when fishing for steelhead or salmon is hooking a chrome rocket on a jig you designed and made yourself. Fortunately, jig making is quite simple and can be done with only a few special tools and materials that are readily available at almost any fly shop. This chapter will take you through the steps of building a basic jig, and the essentials for building more advanced jigs.

THE BASIC JIG

To get started you will need to assemble some basic fly-tying equipment and a few packages of tying materials such as marabou and rabbit strips. Here is a beginner's shopping list:

Fly-tying vise, bobbin, flame red Danville's flat waxed nylon, black Danville's 3/0 waxed monochord, #1 Owner jig hook, #2 Gamakatsu jig hooks, size large & size medium nickel-plated lead eyes, thin Super Glue, toothpicks, marabou, good-quality scissors.

MAKING EYES

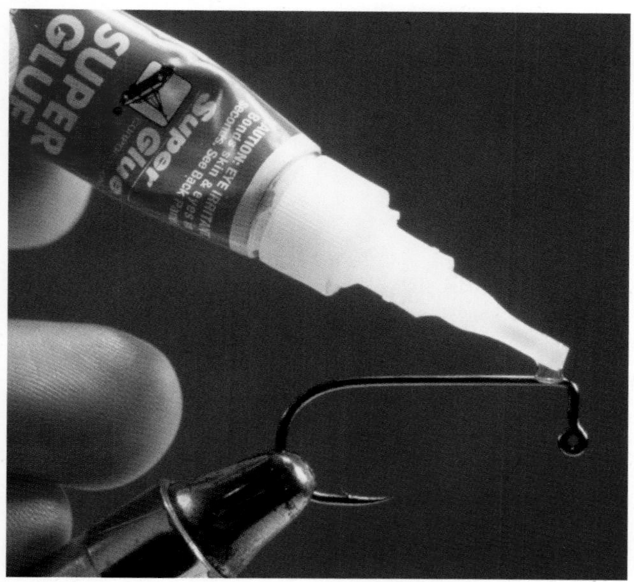

Place the hook in fly-tying vise then put a small drop of Super Glue on the shank.

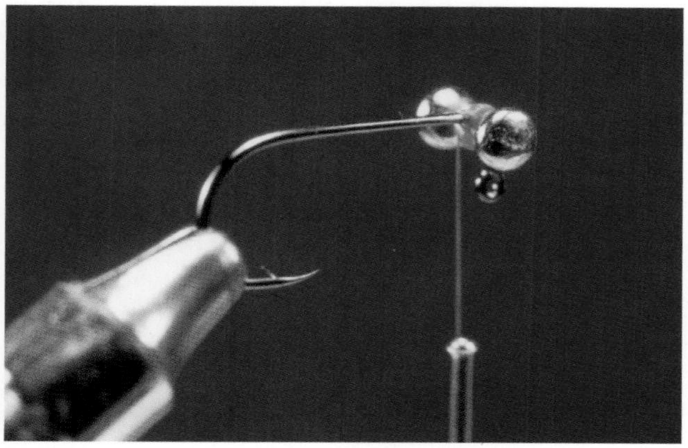

Make a few wraps of tying thread around the hook shank and start wrapping the lead eyes into the "elbow" of the jig hook using figure-eights until you build up a good thread base. The lead eyes can be difficult to secure firmly. Make tight wraps and make a lot of them. Finish off the wraps with a whip finish or a series of at least five very firm half hitches. Coat the warps with a final layer of Super Glue. Reattach the thread just behind the eyes and wind the thread 1/3 the way down the hook shank.

TYING THE MARABOU TAIL

The tips of the marabou plume are the best part of the feather and the easiest with which to work. The average jig uses three pieces of marabou. Cut a tip section about 2 inches long. Arrange the colors in any way that pleases you. Hold the feather firmly against the hook shank and begin winding the thread forward. Trim the excess marabou just behind the lead eyes.

FORMING THE BODY

Wind the thread back and forth, building up a smooth body that tapers larger towards the eyes. Tie off the thread with a half hitch or whip finish. A super knot is not important, as we'll use more Super Glue later.

FINISHING THE JIG

Trim the tail 3/8-inch past the hook bend. Next, apply a light coat of Super Glue to the body, taking care to keep it away from the marabou tail. Spread it evenly with the toothpick. Go easy! If you get Super Glue into the marabou you'll ruin the jig. Hang the jig somewhere to dry, which takes about 5 minutes.

You now have a basic jig. There is nothing fancy about this jig, but it works and works well. Isn't that what we are shooting for?

I have learned that an amazing assortment of colors and color combinations will trick steelhead. In general, I like to use small jigs in 1/32- to 1/8-ounce sizes with pale colors in low, clear water. I prefer larger jigs in the 1/8- to 1/4-ounce size in water with less than six feet of visibility. In that condition I also prefer hot colors. My all-time favorite, go-to color, is cerise. Below is a chart to help you make color selection, but half the fun of jig making is experimenting with colors and materials that please you, and hopefully, the fish.

EXPERIMENTING WITH OTHER MATERIALS

Marabou has long been a staple for jig manufacturers, and for good reason. It has a great undulating action, even in slow water. However, many other materials also work well. Rabbit fur makes an excellent jig, as does schlappen. (Schlappen is a hackle that is soft and wispy. It often comes in a package stitched together in strings.) Somewhat surprisingly, at least to me, bucktail has proven successful for steelhead jigs. In addition, a variety of synthetic products, such as Flashabou, look great on jigs and, in my opinion, work especially well on jigs designed for coho and chinook salmon.

ADVANCED JIGS

Many others and I have a strong preference for jigs that incorporate beads as part of the design. It may be that salmon and steelhead respond to the beads because they resemble salmon eggs or, perhaps they are simply responding to the flash and translucence of the beads, but one thing is certain—jigs with beads work, and work well. To make your own jigs with bead bodies, you will need to assemble the following tools and materials:

11/32-inch brass beads, 1/0 jig hooks, heavy-duty pins, fly-tying bobbin & thread, Super Glue, 6-millimeter fluorescent red plastic beads, 7/64-inch drill bit, pliers, and schlappen hackle. Not pictured: fly-tying vise and cordless drill.

The first step is to slide an 11/32-inch brass bead onto a heavy-duty pin. Take as many wraps of thread as

SIZE & COLOR CHART

Color Combos	Lead Eyes	Hook	Body	Tail Color
		Winter/Spring		
Pink/White	Large	#1 Owner	Red	2 White, 1 Pink
Cerise	Large	#1 Owner	Red	3 Fuchsia
Pink Worm	Large	#1 Owner	Red or Pink	2" Rabbit Strip
Cerise/Purple	Large	#1 Owner	Red or Black	2 Purple, 1 Fuchsia
Orange	Large	#1 Owner	Red	2 Orange, 1 White
Blood Red	Large	#1 Owner	Black	3 Blood Red
Black/Cerise	Large	#1 Owner	Red	2 Cerise, 1 Black
		Summer/Fall		
Black/Cerise	Medium	#2 Gamakatsu	Red	2 Black, 1 Cerise
Blue/White	Medium	#2 Gamakatsu	Black	2 Turquoise, 1 White
Peach	Medium	#2 Gamakatsu	Orange	3 Peach
Purple/Pink	Medium	#2 Gamakatsu	Black	2 Purple, 1 Pink

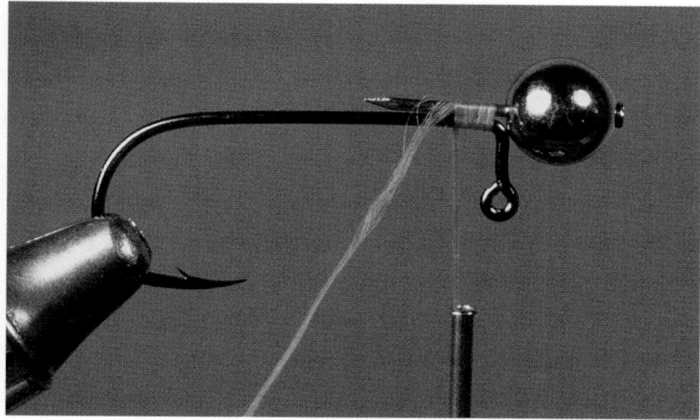

necessary to secure the pin and the bead to the hook shank. Once the pin and bead are securely tied in, coat the thread with super glue.

Make several jig heads and let them dry before moving to the next step.

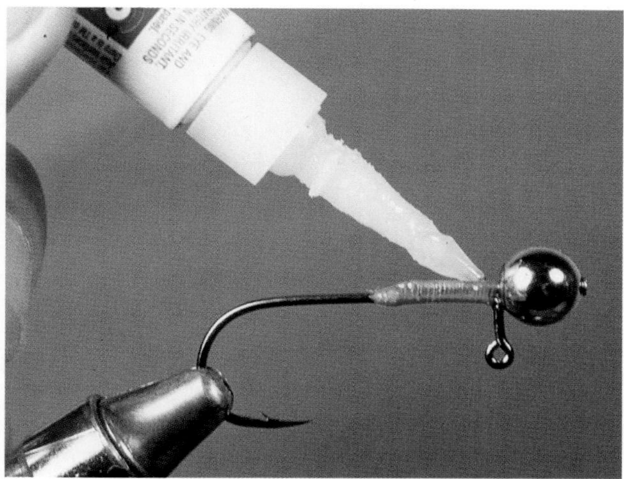

To prepare the plastic bead, grip it with pliers and begin drilling the hole. Set your drill on slow speed. (Be sure to

wear goggles when doing this!) Carefully drill through the bead. I like to drill all the beads I will need before I begin assembling jigs.

Slide one to three beads onto the hook and secure with as many wraps of thread as necessary. Then add body materials such as schlappen, marabou or rabbit fur.

SOME THOUGHTS ON TYING YOUR OWN JIGS

Wrap bead in solidly, then tie in your choice of tail materials.

Wrap the feathers forward and tie off. You now have a high-quality, finished jig.

A year-round selection of his favorite steelhead jigs tied by Dave Kilhefner.

There are many top-quality jigs available at tackle stores and in catalogs. If you consider the value of your time and the cost of materials, you will save little by making your own. The primary reason to build your own is the satisfaction of knowing you fooled that salmon or steelhead with a creation of your own invention. Another good reason to tie your own is to have the freedom to try sizes, colors, and materials that may not be available in commercial products. You will learn in the chapter on tackle that many colors shown to be highly visible to fish are not readily available in commercially tied jigs. Yet another reason to make your own. After all, if it weren't for guys who were willing to experiment, we wouldn't have these awesome lures today. Who knows, maybe that new jig you design may forever change the way we fish.

SUMMARY

- There really are no rules. Make what you like and don't be afraid to try new colors and materials.
- For better visibility, try to use color combinations that provide contrast.
- Use materials that undulate and flash, even in slow water.
- Always use top-quality, razor-sharp hooks.

Todd Kimball caught this native steelhead on a homemade black-and-white jig.

CHAPTER 4

READING WATER

YOU CAN'T CATCH A FISH THAT ISN'T there. It's so obvious that I hate to say it, but nothing is more important than fishing where the fish are. The first step towards success is finding the fish. Usually that involves reading water. Occasionally, you can see steelhead or salmon in their lie. With the salmon fraternity decent, numbers of fish are almost always given away by porpoising or rolling on the surface. Chums typically land on their sides leaving little doubt as to their presence. Coho and pinks usually make a cleaner reentry. When the two are mixed it can be hard to know which is which simply from their surface splash. Chinook typically make such huge swirls that there is no doubt they are the king of the river.

When you spot an undisturbed steelhead or salmon, cast to your quarry and succeed in hooking it, you have experienced one of the higher joys of fishing. Unfortunately, only a small minority of steelhead and salmon are seen before they are hooked. Most of your time will be devoted to fishing where you think the fish ought to be. With a little practice, you can use the clues found on the water's surface to make accurate guesses about your quarry's whereabouts. Learning to interpret these clues is known as reading water.

It has been said, ad nauseam, that 10 percent of the anglers catch 90 percent of the fish. That's probably an overstatement, but not by much. Perhaps a more important, and also totally unscientific, statistic is that 90 percent of the fish are found in 10 percent of the river. The small cadre of anglers who catch most of the fish know which 10 percent of the river is most likely to hold fish. The top rods undoubtedly have other well-honed skills, but there is no avoiding the fact that you can't catch a fish unless you fish where they are. If you understand their needs, you can often predict where steelhead and salmon are holding. Good holding lies can be compared to the best seats in a theater. There may not always be someone in the seat, but if there's a good crowd, you know which seats will be occupied.

Our adversaries have evolved to survive in the highly dangerous environment they inhabit, not through intelligence, but by instinctive wariness. When a native steelhead or salmon has successfully returned to the river, it has beaten very high odds. Its success is due to good instincts. These instincts, shared by all wild salmonoids, cause each fish to act much like all the others in its family tree.

Spawning in the river is a salmonoid's primary goal. On the way to that goal they seek water that provides life's three essentials—safety, food and comfort (comfort relates to current speed, oxygen needs and water temperature.) Water that fully meets all of these needs will hold fish, if decent numbers of fish are in the river. If only two of the three needs are met, fish may or may not be present. If none of these needs are met, fish will be present only briefly as they pass through to more suitable water. When an angler can recognize the surface features that tell them where these three essentials are found, they are well on

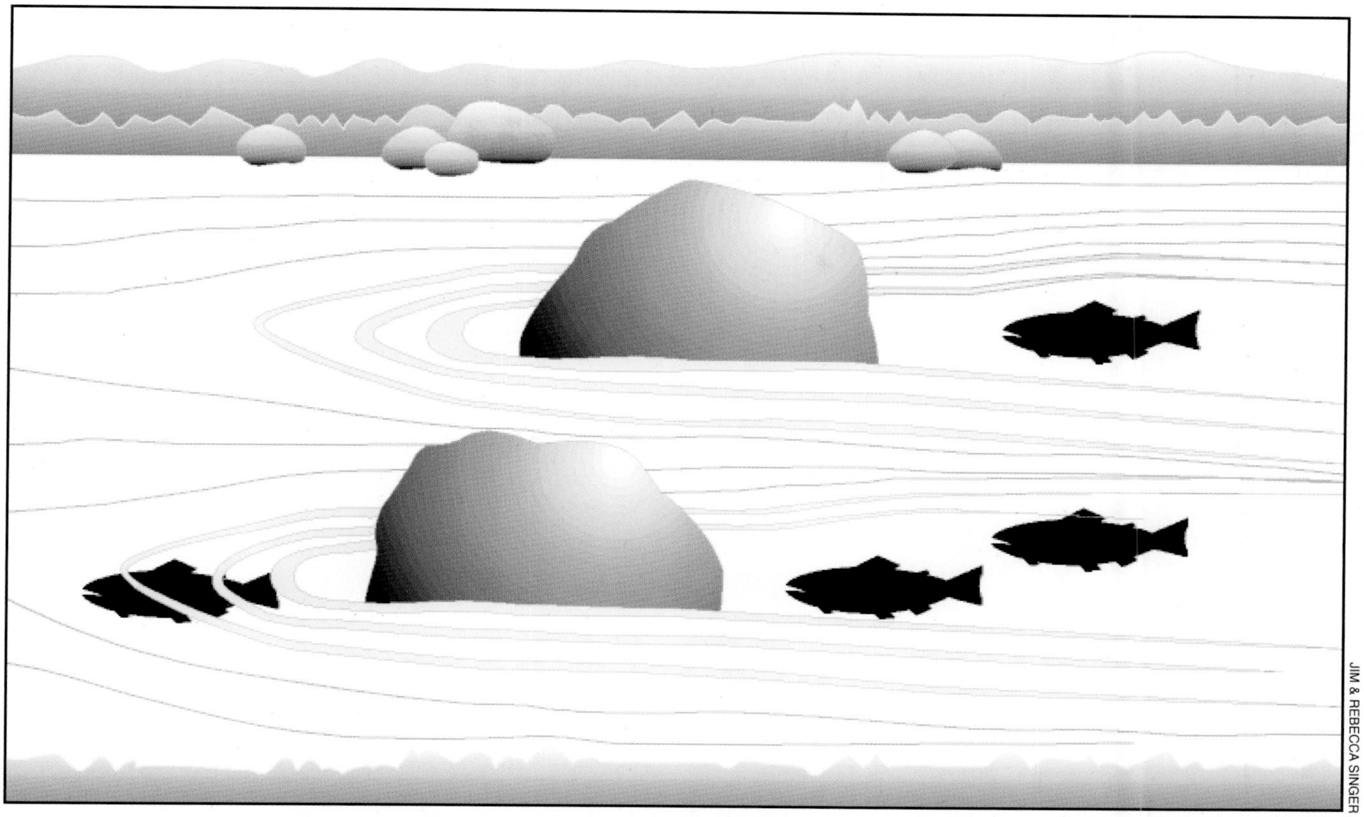

JIM & REBECCA SINGER

In-river structures are one of the first places to look for fish.

their way to learning to read water. One way to begin the search for good holding water is to exclude those areas that are not suitable to a salmonoid's needs.

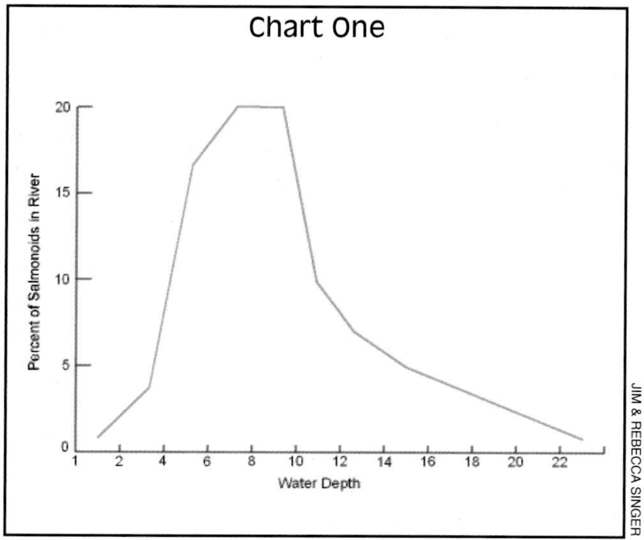

Under normal conditions most members of the steelhead and salmon family will be found in water between three and 12 feet deep.

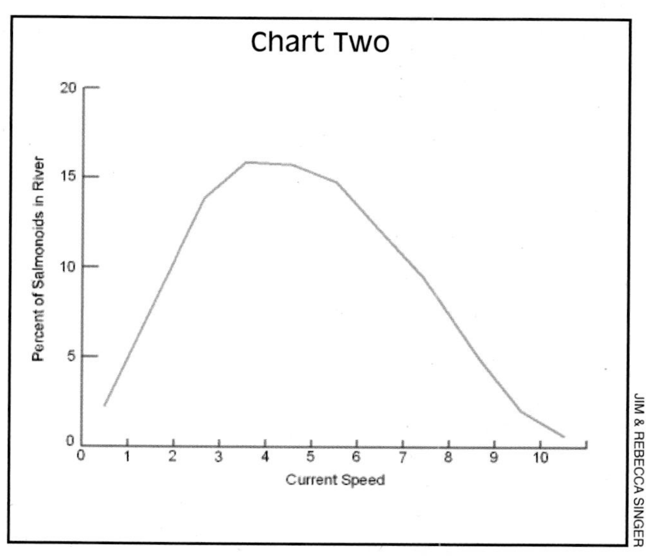

In typical situations, steelhead and salmon will be found in currents between two and eight knots. Exceptions are noted in later chapters, covering specific tactics for each species.

The two charts graphically display the likelihood that steelhead and, to a lesser extent, salmon will be present in the various water depths and current speeds we commonly

Guide John Garrett battles a hot steelhead in a long run. Using a float and dark-colored jig was a stealthy way to cover this run.

encounter. Remember, these are only general rules that have many exceptions. A salmonoid's main concern is security. They will almost always seek water that hides them from their enemies. Water speed, water clarity and water depth all play a role in providing cover for them.

As Chart One shows, the vast majority of steelhead, and most salmon, are found in water between three and ten feet deep. You can usually pass by water outside these parameters, thus avoiding areas with a low probability of holding fish. Chart Two shows that most holding steelhead and salmon, are in water flowing at a rate of between three and six knots. (The primary exceptions are chinook salmon that tend to hold in relatively fast, deep water and coho and pink salmon that will pause on their journey in slow, deep backwaters and sloughs.) Three knots equate to a brisk walk, six knots is equivalent to a fast jog. If you begin your search by eliminating very shallow water, very deep water, very slow water, and very fast water, you have eliminated a large percentage of the river that seldom holds fish.

There are obvious exceptions to these rules. For example, many small rivers have almost no water deeper than three feet. Yet, even here, most fish are found in the pockets that offer a good combination of depth and current speed. The combination of water depth, current speed, and, to a lesser extent, oxygen levels dictate the likelihood that a salmonid will be present in an area. Normally, you will not find salmonids holding in water less than three feet deep—the exception being when a rapid current flow provides enough chop and bubbles to hide the fish. These rapid runs also provide added oxygen needed by low-water summer fish. Conversely, you seldom find a steelhead in dead water with a current flow of less than one knot—the exception being when water depths of eight feet or more obscure the fish from your view. Steelhead, coho and chinook will often stack in such deep pools in extremely cold weather. (As previously mentioned, coho love to hold, sometimes for days, in water that is quite slow and deep.)

Unlike salmon, the steelhead's second concern relates to feeding. Some argue that steelhead do not eat after returning to the river as adults. This is simply not true. Anyone who has seen a summer steelhead take a dry fly or a winter fish swallow an egg cluster, knows that adult steelhead feed, sometimes aggressively. Steelhead may feed less aggressively in rivers than they did in the ocean, but that is due, at least in part, to the relative lack of food in our rivers.

On the Stamp River in the winter of 1990 I saw a small hen steelhead take a variety of baits and lures in a fifteen-minute period. We had been fishing a seam where the fast, deep water at the outside of a bend met the slower water at the inside of the bend. As our floats trotted down the seam, repeatedly we would see a strike but just couldn't seem to get a solid hookup. We began by using spawn sacks, switched to sand shrimp and switched again to pink rubber worms. Finally, my float went down, and I set the hook on a small chrome-bright fish. After a quick battle we netted it and as it lay flopping on the bottom of our boat, the hen spit out two spawn sacks and two sand shrimp. In addition, it had struck at my rubber worm, which proved to be its downfall. This was a winter fish that was feeding aggressively.

Both steelhead and salmon love to hold in water where fast and slow currents come together. Serious anglers have long known that these seams, or creases as the English call them, are superlative holding water. Seams are caused by a variety of river conditions, including points jutting into the river, shallow flats dropping suddenly into deeper slots, river bends, rocks, bridge abutments, snags, and other obstructions that significantly change the current flow. Seams are sometimes marked by foam lines and are usually readily apparent by the distinct line where slick water abuts the choppy riffled water.

In high water, steelhead and salmon are usually found on the slow side of seams where they can avoid strong currents and find cleaner water. Low-water fish lie on the fast side of the seam where oxygen levels are higher and the rippled surface provides cover. In rivers with five feet or more of visibility you will often find fish holding just a

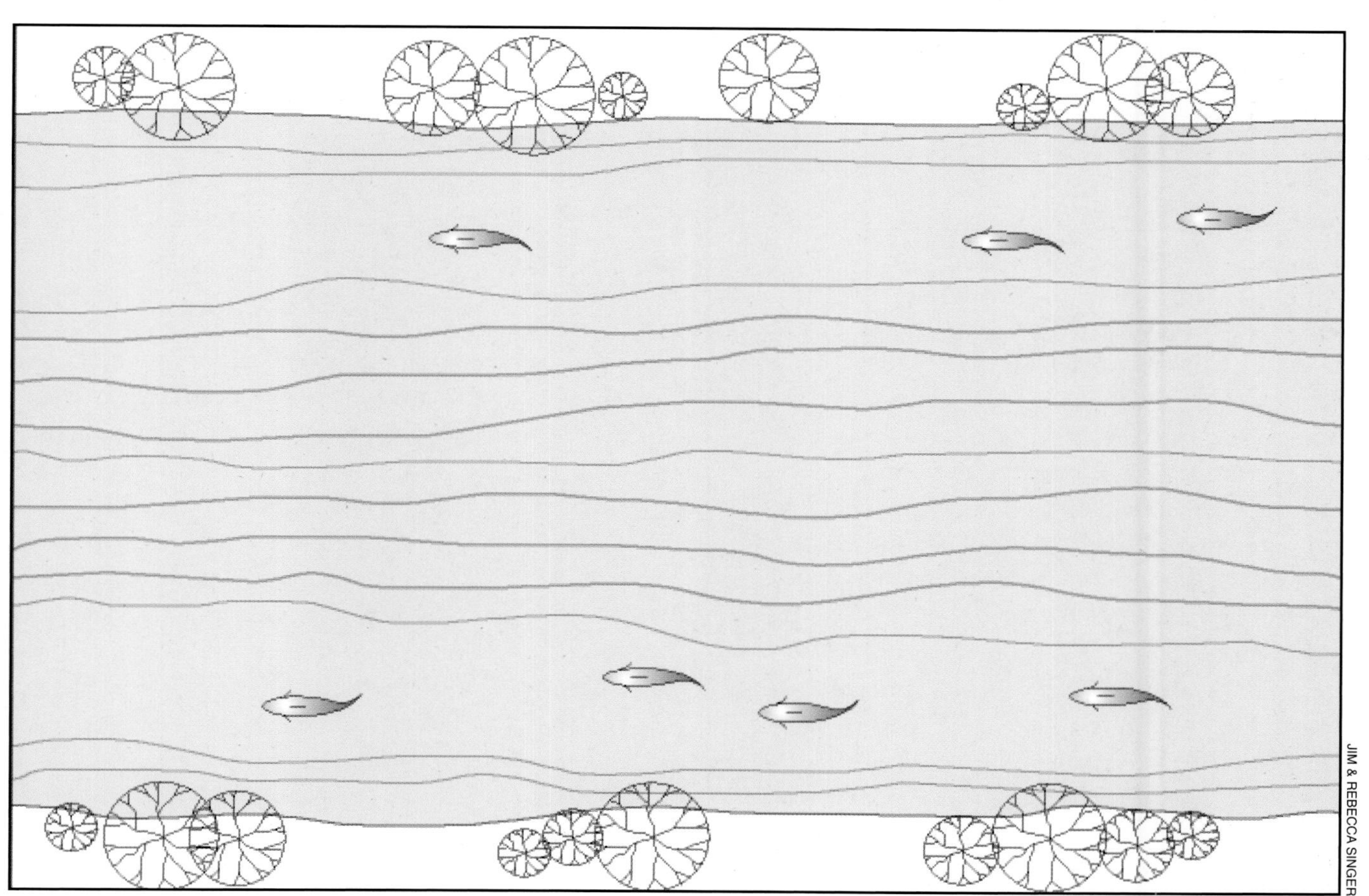

Steelhead will almost always be in seams where fast and slow currents converge.

bit deeper than the horizon where you lose sight of the bottom. I usually make my first cast to this area, working my jig along a line just beyond where the bottom drops out of sight.

Most salmonoids will hold at the edge of current flows, usually relatively near shore.

Working seams with a float and jig is child's play. If the seam is caused by an in-stream obstruction, such as a bridge abutment, boulder or snag, simply cast a bit upstream of the obstruction and work your float down the entire length of the seam. Work the seams on both sides of mid-stream obstructions and then work the area directly in front of and behind the obstruction. There will be a back-eddy on both sides of the obstruction. Often steelhead hold just behind rock and other obstructions where the back-eddy begins to weaken.

Fish will often be found behind or in front of in-river structures.

Seams caused by river contours, such as curves, drop-offs and points, are also easy. If possible, position yourself above the head of the seam and drift your float down the length of the seam. On the fast side of the seam, let your float drift at the speed of the surface current for two or three drifts, then try a few drifts holding back just a bit, to slow the lure to a speed near that of the bottom current. On the slow side of the seam let your float dance along at the whim of the current.

Seams are not a constant in a river. In times of extreme high water, seams may be found within a few feet of the bank where shoreside bushes and stream contours slow the rushing water. If the visibility is two feet or more, a jig worked near the shore will yield fish in a river many would consider un-fishable. Even experienced anglers often overlook these prime seams because they are used to looking for fish closer to the middle of the river. Conversely, in very low water the fish may move from their usual haunts to find shelter in pockets as small as a bathtub. But remember, even these small pockets will invariably be marked by a seam on one or both sides.

Comfort is the last of the salmonoid's primary needs, but it is an important factor in deciding where they hold. To illustrate how fish use current breaks for comfort, a good analogy would be that of a man crossing a field in a windstorm. The man soon discovers that trees and buildings provide respite from the wind. A smart man will move from one windbreak to another as he crosses the field. It's much the same with salmonoids working their way upriver. They duck behind rocks, snags and other obstructions to rest before continuing upstream. Savvy anglers look for these rest stops, as in the illustration below.

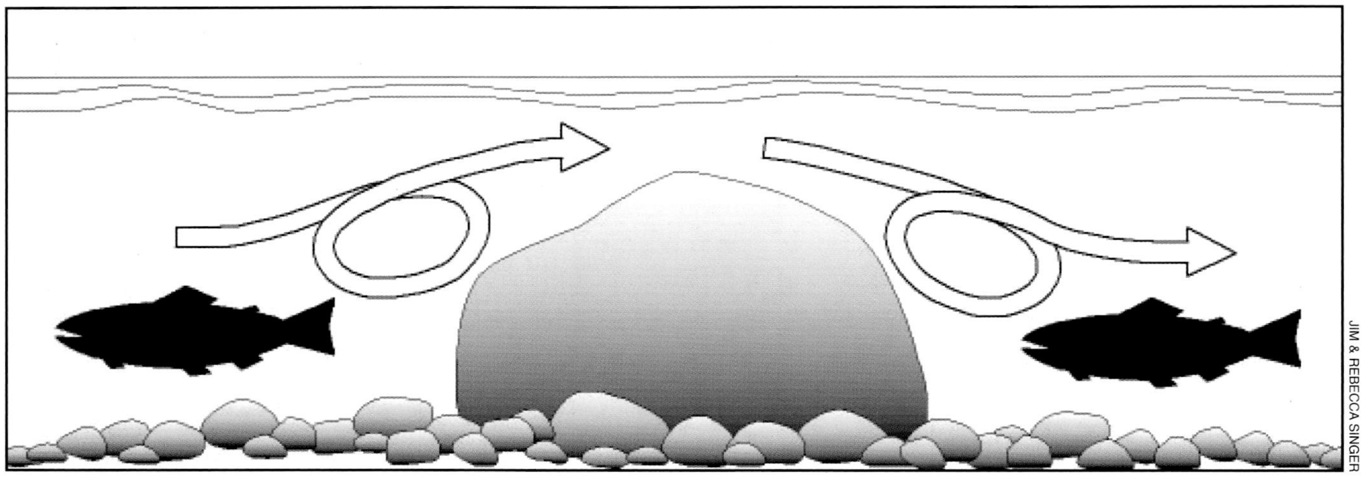
JIM & REBECCA SINGER

In instances of extreme water temperature, flood conditions or drought, comfort considerations force fish to move to lies they would not normally use. If river flows diminish to the point that the fish's oxygen needs are not fully met, the fish move to whitewater riffles and cascades where oxygen is more abundant. They do this even if these areas do not provide the optimum degree of safety. Conversely, when rivers are near flood stage, salmonoids move to the edges, sometimes literally into the bushes, where they find cleaner water and the comfort of the slower current.

As water temperatures rise above their comfort range, fish seek pools near the mouth of tributaries and lie near the bottom in the cool water found there. Chinook salmon are famous for stacking up at the mouth of clean tributaries, even if they are not headed up that tributary.

In extremely cold water, steelhead tend to hold near the bottom in deep, slow pools. Here they find the security of

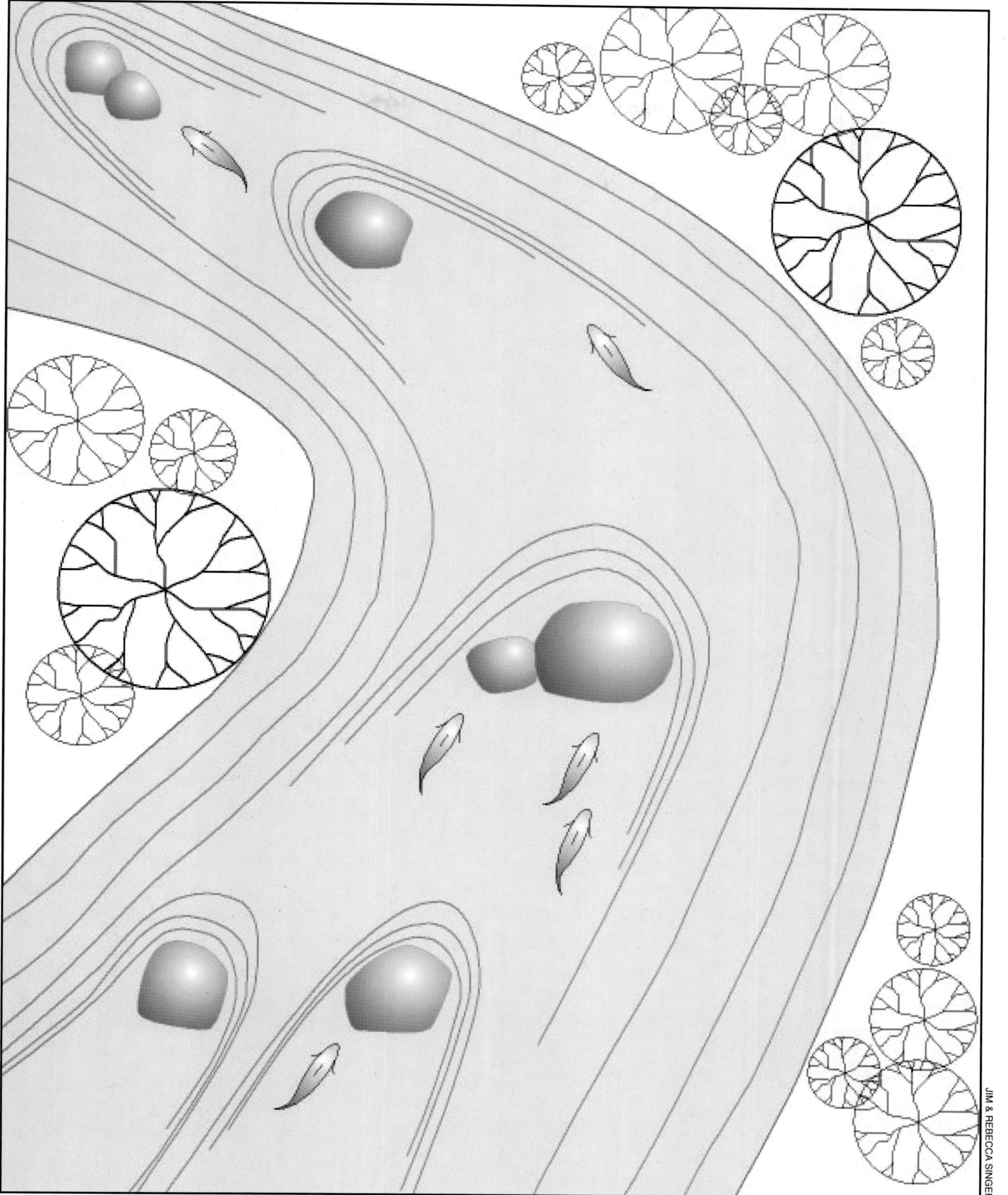

JIM & REBECCA SINGER

Steelhead and salmon love to hold in soft water caused by rock or logs in the river.

Fish will often stack up behind obstructions of fast-water chutes.

deep water and expend little effort as they become almost dormant in the still water. Most anglers find steelhead difficult to tempt under these conditions, but a jig slowly undulating past their lie is often rewarded with a strike.

When you hook a salmon or steelhead, try to remember two things. First, remember the exact spot where you found the fish. On another day, if river conditions are similar, there is a strong chance another fish will be in that lie. Second, note the attributes of the spot in which you found your fish. How deep was the run? Was there any structure in the lie that provided a current break? Was the current choppy, slick, and white with bubbles? How fast was the current? What did the surface look like? If you note the characteristics of a known lie, you will likely notice other areas with similar attributes. Now you know what some of the seats in the theater are like.

There is a good deal more to reading water than these few simple paragraphs. Entire books have been written on the topic, and, even then, the authors could not cover all the variables of water temperature, run timing, river height, water clarity, seasonality, and a dozen other factors that keep our sport unpredictable and exciting. Reading water is a skill that you will never perfect, but constant observation improves your stream literacy.

SUMMARY

- Target high-percentage water that consistently holds fish.
- Quickly pass through areas that are not prime lies.
- Look for lies that offer the fish comfort and security.
- Constantly observe the river's surface for clues as to what lies beneath.

John Garrett shows off one of many jig-caught steelhead hooked in this eastern Washington river.

5 CHAPTER

JIG-FISHING TACKLE

I HAVE SEEN GREAT ANGLERS, USING substandard tackle, outfish poor anglers with excellent tackle. But to enjoy the sport to its utmost, and increase your chances of making contact with a steelhead or salmon, you need appropriate tackle, which is not to say that you must have expensive tackle. Jig fishermen essentially have three ways to fish jigs: with a float, as a stand-alone lure, or with a fly rod. As this book is not aimed at fly-fishers, I will cover only the first two methods.

THE JIG-AND-FLOAT COMBINATION

When targeting steelhead, chum salmon and chinook salmon, most of us prefer to fish the jig under a float. This calls for a long rod, a float, a weighting system and a jig. First let's discuss your choices in rods.

No other element of your jig-fishing tackle is as important as your rod. Success with jig-fishing demands that you are able to make accurate casts to distant lies and do so with as much as ten feet of line beneath your float. (You may use considerably shorter rods if fishing without a float or in certain special situations.) This dictates a long rod, in most instances a rod of ten feet or longer. Those who have never fished with a float and jig may think 10-foot rods are ridiculously long. But those who have fished floats and jigs for years usually own several rods in the 10- to 12-foot range.

The reasons for long rods are numerous. Perhaps the most important reason to use such a long rod is the need to keep your line off the water. As I discuss in the chapter on techniques, it is imperative when fishing for steelhead, chum salmon and chinook salmon that your jig is presented

Often simplicity is the key to success. Sometime a fixed rig is all you need. Note the plastic sleeves on the top and bottom of this balsa float. You can quickly adjust your depth by sliding the float up and down the line.

An early May hatchery summer steelhead that fell for a hot-pink jig. It's important to keep your jigs well organized.

as naturally as possible. This means you cannot have any drag caused by current tugging on your line. There are several ways to get a drag-free drift, but keeping your line off the water is one of the most effective ways to eliminate drag.

Another reason for a long rod is to allow you to fish relatively deep water with a fixed float. Consider what happens when you try to fish a 10-foot-deep lie with a float using a standard 9-foot steelhead rod. You must slide your float up the line until you have something in the range of eight feet or more of line between the float and the jig. Now you find that your 9-foot rod is too short to keep your jig off the ground. If your line is dragging in the dirt before you begin your cast, disaster awaits you.

Now let's imagine that you have somehow managed to cast your float and jig to that fishy-looking seam on the far side of the run with your 9-foot rod. Even if you stand on a rock and hold your hands above your head, you can't keep the line off the water. As the currents tug at the line lying on the water, a belly will form in the line. Soon the line will be pulling the float to the side or pulling it downstream at an unnatural pace.

If, in this imaginary scenario, you somehow managed to get your jig to the run you wanted to fish, and if you somehow managed to draw a strike, your short rod would still be your undoing. Because the rod is too short to keep your line off the water, you cannot avoid a significant amount of slack between your rod tip and the float. When the float goes down, you haul back mightily on the rod only to yank a few feet of slack line toward you. The float hasn't moved, and the fish is now gone.

There is no way to avoid it. You are going to have to buy at least one rod that is 10 feet or longer. Later, when you have been fully hooked on jigs and floats, you may want to try even longer rods, but the 10 1/2-foot rod is a fine all-purpose float-and-jig rod.

RODS FOR BAIT-CASTING REELS

If you are fishing big water and you have no way to get close to where you want to fish, a bait-casting rod and reel is the way to go. The bait-caster is ideal for fishing when the combined weight of your terminal gear, float, weight and jig, weighs more than 3/8 of an ounce.

A few years ago, good float rods designed for bait-casting reels were hard to find in the US. Fortunately, several US manufacturers make a fine selection of float rods. Today Lamiglas manufactures the Dave Vedder signature series of rods that I designed specifically for fishing with floats. G. Loomis has a great selection and some of the lightest float rods on the market. Their only drawback is a stiff price. In addition, Shimano makes a line of inexpensive rods that will serve the purpose.

The optimum bait-casting rod for float-and-jig-fishing should have a strong backbone and still have enough sensitivity to telegraph strikes. Even though your float can act as a strike indicator, you will find that you can often feel the take as well as see it. An ideal float rod for winter steelhead, chums, and chinook should be rated for 10- to 20-pound-test line. It should weigh as little as possible and be well balanced to avoid fatigue. The handle length from the center of the reel seat to the butt plate should be at least 13 inches to give you the leverage for long casts. Those of you who graduate to center-pin reels will need to select rods with longer fore grips and shorter handles. I believe an ideal float-and-jig rod for summer-run steelhead, pink salmon, and coho will be rated for 8- to 12-pound-test line, will be between 10 and 12 feet in length and will have a fast action.

SPINNING RODS

In the past few years, spinning rods have dramatically increased in popularity with jig-fishers. In several ways, spinning rods are superior to bait-casting rods and in a few ways they are inferior. I believe any serious angler will outfit themselves with both styles of rod so they are ready for whatever conditions they encounter. I prefer a bait-caster for fishing where I need to make long casts and need to use relatively heavy combinations of weight and jig. But whenever I can fish effectively with relatively short casts, I prefer a spinning rod. One of the biggest advantages of spinning rods is the ability of spinning reels to cast very light weights. This means that with a spinning reel you can fish small jigs and small floats and cast them a decent distance.

A superb low-water combination is a small float with little or no weight between the float and a small jig. If the fish are very spooky, a 6-pound-test main line, a small float, 4-pound-test leader and a small jig is a deadly combination. Unfortunately, most bait-casting reels and most center-pin reels will not cast such lightweight terminal gear. A spinning reel will, but at a price.

The spinning reel will deliver a lighter package than any other reel, but it can be difficult to use when drifting floats to downstream positions. To free-spool with a spinning reel the bail must be in the open position. When the bail is open it is hard to make a fast, solid hook-set. For an open-bail hook-set, you have two choices: You can trap the line between your fingers and the fore grip or spool before setting the hook, or you can take the time to crank the reel handle to flip the bail back closed. Both methods have drawbacks. Trapping the line beneath your fingers may prove to be difficult if you are wearing gloves or if your fingers are cold. Flipping the bail takes precious time, and unless you have the drag set very tight, you may still not get a solid hook-set. If you choose to keep your drag tight to assure a solid hook-set, you will need to act fast to loosen the drag as soon as you have a good hook-up.

In spite of its drawbacks, a long, light rod rigged with a spinning reel is the optimum set-up for low-water, spooky steelhead. Like democracy, it's far from perfect, but it's the best we have.

Today there are many fine spinning reels on the market that will suit the jig fisherman quite well. Because I only use spinning reels in places where small jigs, small floats and light lines are necessary, I prefer a spinning rod rated for 4- to10-pound-test line. Because a fast action is not useful for casting light jigs, I prefer medium to slow action in a spinning rod. The best length would be between 9 and 11 feet.

RODS FOR FISHING JIGS WITHOUT A FLOAT

When fishing for coho and pink salmon it is usually best to fish your jig without a float. The reasons for this will be discussed in detail in the chapter on salmon-fishing techniques. Occasionally you will want to fish steelhead, chum salmon, and chinook salmon without a float. When you opt to take off the float and fish 'naked,' you will want to switch rods as well. Because jig-fishing without a float does not require that you make an effort to achieve a natural drift, a long rod is not mandatory. However, after years of fishing long rods, I have discovered that even when a long rod is not absolutely necessary for a drag-free drift, long rods do provide the benefit of better hook-sets, better line control and longer casts.

RODS FOR FISHING JIGS

Often when fishing for coho and chinook, you will be fishing jigs weighing 1/4 ounce or more. In those cases I recommend using a bait-casting reel coupled with a rod in the 9- to 10-foot range. For coho, steelhead and average-sized chums; I recommend a fast-action bait-casting rod rated for line in the 8- to 12-pound range.

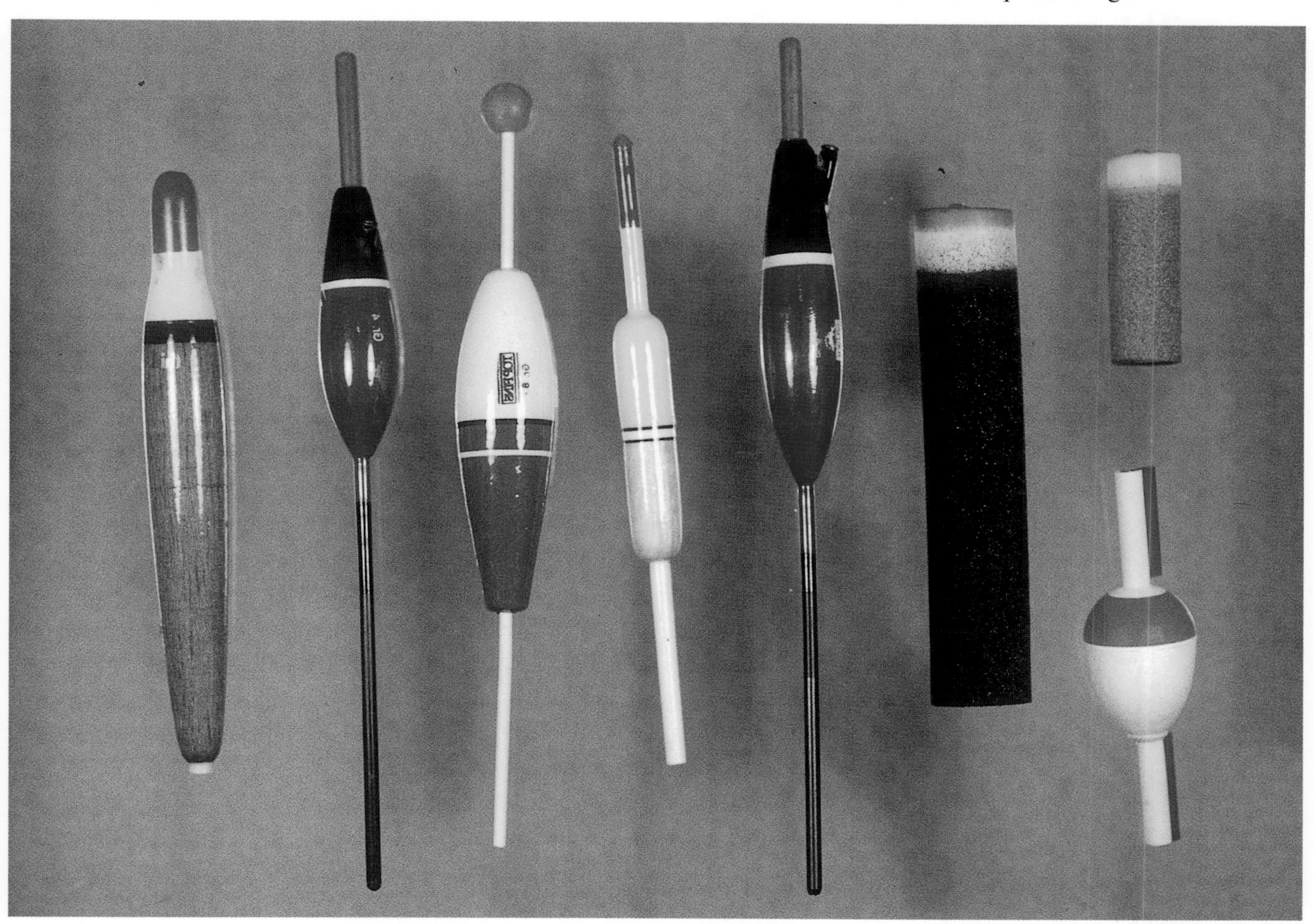

Today's floats come in sizes and styles appropriate for any situation we might encounter.

If you plan to target big steelhead, big chums or chinook salmon you will want a bait-casting rod nine to ten feet long, with a medium-fast action, rated for lines in the 10- to 20-pound-test range.

Many times, when fishing a jig without a float, you will be using small jigs. This is especially true when fishing summer-run steelhead and pink salmon. For this work your best bet will be a spinning rod and reel. This is because bait casters are not designed to cast jigs weighing less than 1/4 ounce. It can be done, but for most of us, using a bait-caster with weights of less than 1/4 ounce results in bird's nests, short casts and frustration. For tossing the lighter jigs, I recommend a lightweight rod much like I recommend for fishing small floats and jigs. The good news is you should be able to use the same spinning rod and reel when working with a float or without. If you do want to add another rod to your arsenal, I recommend one that has a medium-fast to fast-action. When fishing without a float, you will be relying on feel to signal a strike. A fast-action rod will telegraph a subtle strike considerably better than a slow-action rod. I prefer a spinning rod rated for 4- to ten-pound-test line. The best length would be between 8 and 10 feet.

REELS

Jig-fishing places no special demands on a reel. Any reel you might use for fishing other lures should work well. There are, however, some jig-fishing situations that dictate specific types of reels. The two primary concerns for a reel are that it allows free-spooling with very little resistance to assure a drag-free drift and that the reel has a smooth drag to help fight the fish.

CENTER-PIN REELS

The center-pin reel is by far the favorite of the serious British Columbia and Great Lakes steelheader. This may be because it casts more smoothly than other reels, and because the direct-drive reels require more skill on the angler's part than does a reel with gears. Or it may simply be a badge of competency that announces that this angler is a serious steelheader.

The center-pin reel is a bundle of good and bad that can only be judged by each of us individually. On the plus side of the ledger, these reels are extraordinarily smooth casting. They are usually quite nicely finished, and they allow you to free-spool your float with almost no drag. On the negative side, they can be the devil to learn to cast. The lack of gears makes it difficult to catch up to a fish that is running toward you and, likewise, they retrieve line more slowly than a typical reel with gears. This can cost a steelheader a good deal of time during a full day's angling. In addition, they are usually expensive. Still, there's nothing quite the same as palming a single-action reel while a big steelhead races downstream, then reeling frantically to catch up when the fish reverses course. If you think you are a real pro with a level-wind reel, try the center-pin. At first it will humble you, then it will thrill you.

FLOATS

Almost every jig-fishing situation calls for a float. But there is far more to successfully working a jig than simply attaching your jig beneath a red-and-white plastic bobber. To fish jigs most effectively, you must have a balanced system of rod, reel, float, weights and terminal tackle, all selected to work in harmony.

There is no one best float for jig-fishing, just as there is no one best rod, reel, or jig. Selecting the proper float requires that you give consideration to the type of water you will be fishing, and the combined weight of the jig and lead you intend to fish.

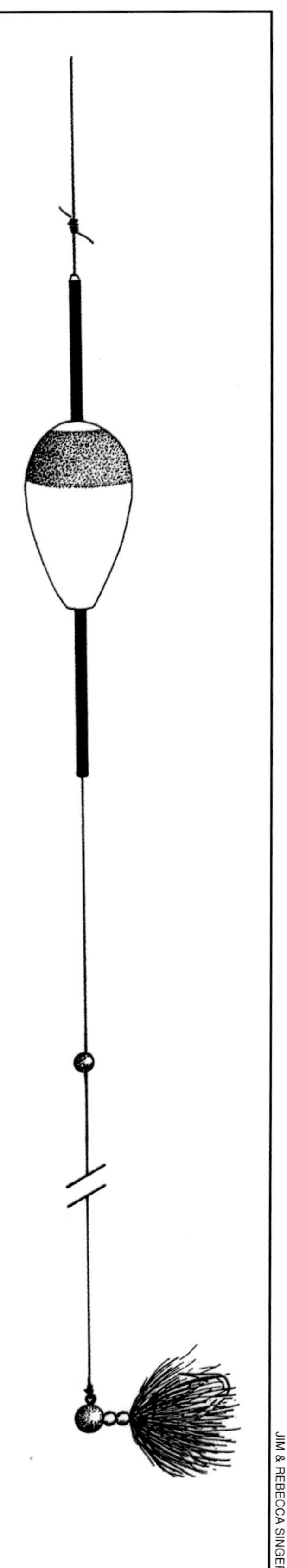

JIM & REBECCA SINGER

There are many floats available today. In addition, many serious jig anglers make their own floats from a variety of materials.

Two of the best steelhead floats are the simple foam floats widely used in British Columbia known as 'dink' floats, and the balsa floats commonly used in the Great Lakes region and now rapidly gaining popularity in the Northwest. Both share the attributes of being infinitely and rapidly adjustable, and both come in a sufficient variety of sizes and shapes to suit almost any fishing situation.

The dink float is inexpensive and can easily be modified to suit almost any water condition. Most dink floats are four to six inches in length, approximately one half inch in diameter and feature a brightly painted top for ease of visibility. Favorite colors are red, orange and chartreuse. Orange and red are most easily seen in low-light conditions, and chartreuse is supposed to best in the middle of the day. Personally I seldom find chartreuse the best color too see on the water. The top of most dink floats is painted with two bands of bright color. The top band marks the ideal water level for fishing quiet waters. The bottom band marks the proper float height for fast water.

Most dink floats are threaded onto the line via a center tunnel or angled tubes at each end of the float. Center

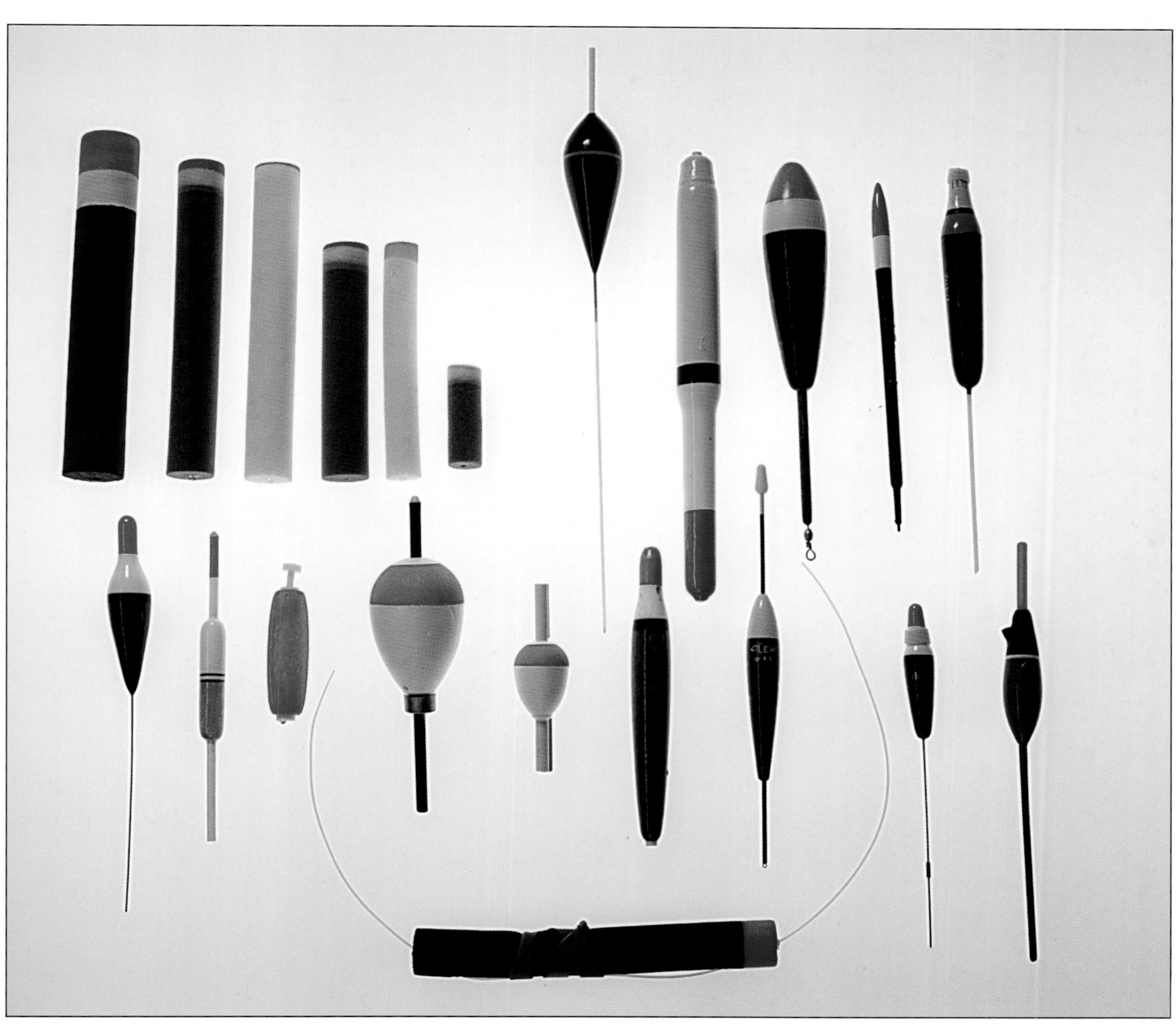

There are many sizes and styles of floats available today. Try to choose the smallest float that will carry your jig appropriately and will cast well.

tunnel tubes are held in place by either a toothpick or a thin bamboo reed that comes with the float. Floats with angled tubes at top and bottom rely on a wrap of line around the float to create sufficient friction to hold the float in place. A great trick is to run your main line through the tube or tubes in the float, but do not make the usual wrap around the float. Then, tying your line to the weight or jig, take a large rubber band and wrap it around the float as many times as necessary to tightly trap the line against the float. This will give you a float that is easily adjustable. And this system will not cut your float in half with a big fish or a hang up. Another plus of the rubber band is that when you break off your terminal gear, you will still get your float back.

Among dink floats, I prefer the dense foam models to the lighter and softer versions. The dense foam floats will carry more weight, will last longer than the soft-foam floats and retain their painted surfaces better.

Today's float anglers have a large variety of floats from which to choose. Always try to use the smallest float that will adequately carry the weight and jig you wish to fish.

Balsa floats are the most lovely of the floats and many prefer the buoyancy of balsa to foam. They are a pleasure to fish, and they are often beautifully finished. Balsa floats come in a variety of sizes ranging from the dime-sized Thill River Master to the six-inch Big Fish Slider. Many balsa floats are designed to be quickly interchangeable, and most are held to the line by silicone sleeves that can quickly be removed to change floats. The top of most balsa floats is painted with two bands of bright color. The top band marks the ideal water level for fishing quiet waters. The bottom of the yellow band marks the proper float height for fast water.

SLIP FLOATS VERSUS FIXED FLOATS

There are some anglers who always use slip floats, and some who always use fixed floats. Top anglers know that different circumstances require different floats. The smart angler uses both types and changes as necessary for the conditions encountered.

When fishing runs that are less than eight feet deep, most anglers prefer the fixed float. Its advantages are that it is easily rigged, fishes the instant it hits the water and you can hold back on the float, if desired, without your jig slipping up toward the surface.

When fishing waters more than eight feet deep, many top anglers prefer the slip float. Its advantage is that you can reach bottom in almost any water, no matter how deep. The slip float's principle disadvantages are that it requires more time to affix to the line because you must somehow attach a float stop and a bead or some other sort of stopper. Slip floats often take a few seconds for the line to slip to the pre-set depth before you are fishing where you want to be, and slip floats will allow the line to slip out of the strike zone if you hold back on the float.

Your best bet is to carry both types of floats and to use the one that best fits the circumstances you find.

Slip floats can be rigged to allow for maximum and minimum depth.

WEIGHTING YOUR FLOAT

There are as many ways to weight a float system as the imagination allows, but all have these important attributes: The float must be weighted so that it protrudes only slightly above the water, and the jig must work its magic near the river bottom. How those attributes are achieved is less important than assuring that those two imperatives are met. However, I do not care for the weighted floats. I find that the weighted floats tend to cause less than subtle splashdowns that may scare fish, and they offer less flexibility than un-weighted floats. You can adjust the weight on a dink float or a balsa float from almost zero weight to as much weight as the float will carry. With a float that has a built-in weight you very likely cannot decrease the weight and if you try to increase the weight, the float may not sit right in the water.

The weights used to properly balance a float are usually split shot ranging in size from the largest magnum shot to fine dust. Shot are ideal weights as they can be added and deleted as needed until the float sits properly in the water. In recent years many float anglers have experimented with small-eared sinkers that have the added benefit of rapid removal, and may be reused repeatedly. The rubber-cored removable sinkers also work well. If you carry three sizes, you can quickly adjust to almost any water condition.

Several weighting systems can be employed to properly weight your jig and float. Your choice depends on water clarity and current speed. In slow, clear water use a system that keep the weights as unobtrusive as possible.

Other weighting systems including pencil lead, slinkeys and hollow-core lead. All have proven to be satisfactory. My favorite system is an in-line slinkey. I

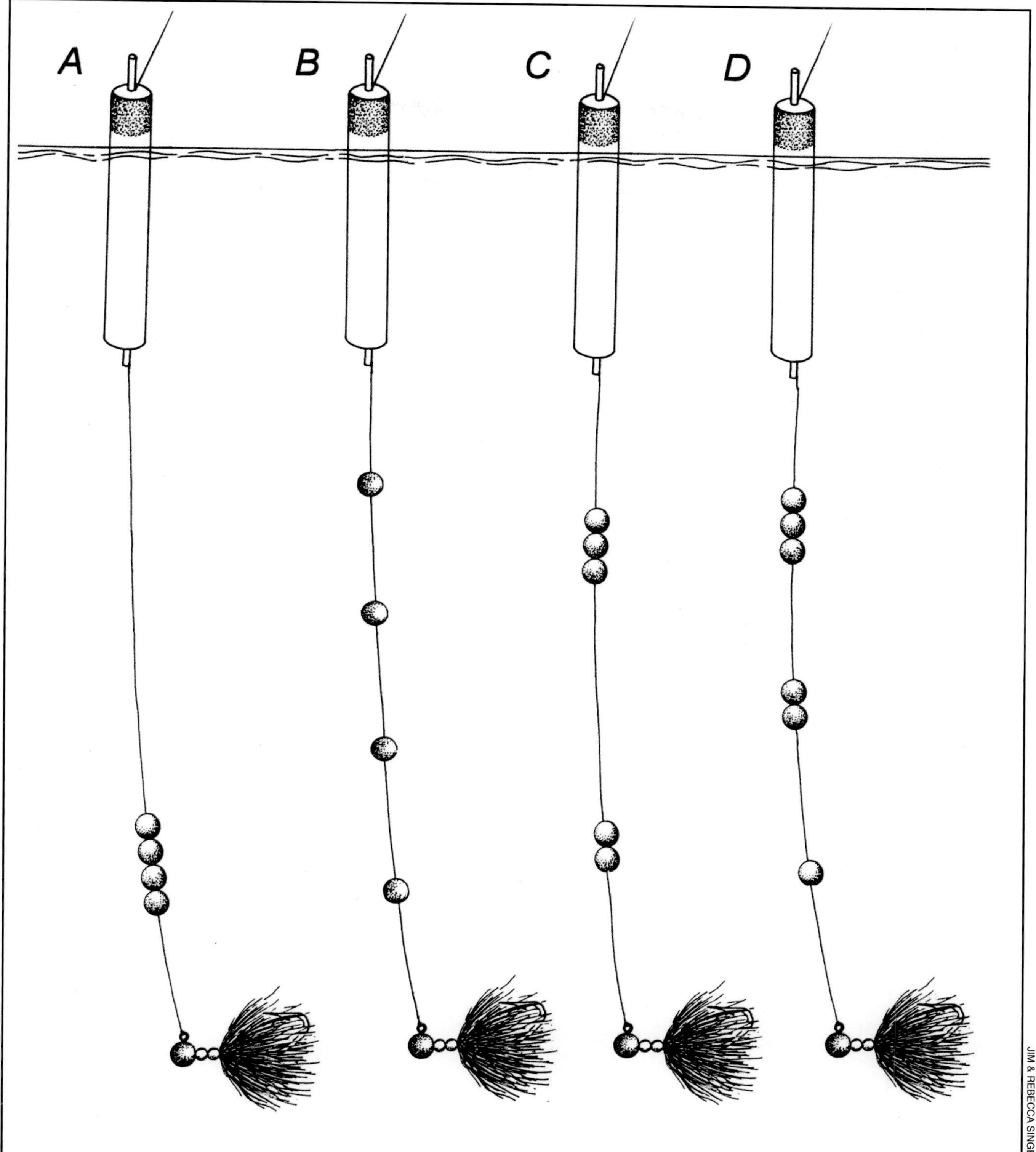

JIM & REBECCA SINGER

simply attach a snap swivel to each end of a slinky and tie my main line to one swivel and the leader to the other. This system seldom hangs up and I can change slinkeys rapidly by simply unsnapping two swivels.

In normal water conditions an in-line slinkey or a piece of hollow pencil lead is an effective weighting method. This system allows you to change weights quickly and it is almost snag-proof.

MAIN LINE

Few other topics will draw as many, and as varied, opinions as the choice of the best main line. In large part the choice is personal preference. The primary consideration is whether to go with the new woven fiber lines or the old standby, monofilament. In my opinion it's hard to beat monofilament when fishing with a bait-casting rod and reel. Monofilament has a lot of stretch when compared to spun fiber lines and that is usually a good thing. That stretch can help solve over-aggressive hooksets and I believe the stretch makes it easier on a fish that we plan to release. In addition, monofilament comes off a bait-casting reel smoothly without the sudden jerks and hesitations often encountered when using spun-fiber lines.

For spinning reels, the newer spun-fiber lines can be excellent. They will allow longer casts, they seem to roll off spinning reels with very little hesitation and they allow much smaller diameter lines as compared to monofilament. The spun-fiber lines often require special knots, but they all seem to work well with the Palomar knot, which is also a great knot for monofilament.

I suggest that you begin with a good-quality monofilament on your bait-casting reel and try a spun-fiber line on your spinning reel. The new Berkley Ironsilk superpolymer lines perform well on both bait-casters and spinning reels. But I recognize there is no right answer when it comes to choosing a main line. Go with what you like and what you are confident in.

BeauMac Marabou Jigs.

LEADERS

Leaders used for jig-fishing run the gamut from 20-pound-test to 2-pound-test and 14 inches long to eight feet long. In the big, colored waters of western rivers, short, heavy leaders work well and are often necessary to land big fish in fast water. In the more gentle waters of Great Lakes rivers, it is usually necessary to go with long, light leaders to draw a strike.

Abrasion-resistant, non-visible material is usually best for leaders. Ande Tournament, Berkley Vision, Berkley XT and Stren Clear Blue Fluorescent are my favorites. When fishing with light leaders where a natural presentation is important go with a limp leader such as Berkley XL.

A good rule of thumb is to use as light a leader as possible for the conditions you find. I believe a limp, light leader will let the jig dance and drift more naturally, bringing you more strikes.

JERRY FERRO

A beautiful selection of salmon and steelhead jigs manufactured by Angler's Advantage.

JIGS, FROM PLAIN TO FANCY

Jigs can be as simple as a tuft of yarn on a hook with lead eyes, to some spectacular hand-tied version that would rival an Atlantic salmon fly. The primary variables in jigs are size, color, and materials used. While the possibilities are infinite, to begin with, you need to choose a jig that is the right size for the water you will be fishing, the right color for the water conditions and a material you have faith in.

Size and color are by far the most important variables. In general, when fishing western rivers with visibility ranging from three feet to six feet, I choose a 1/8- or 1/4-ounce jig. The more visibility, the smaller the jig.

For the body of jigs I prefer something that will wiggle even in almost dead water. My favorite materials are marabou, hackle, rabbit fur and schlappen. Yet I must admit that many steelhead and salmon have been hooked on bucktail jigs and yarn-body jigs that have no sexy wiggle to them.

Today, there are many small tackle companies making some really excellent jigs. There is not room in this book to show all the jigs manufactured today, but I have presented a sampling of what you can find. In addition, if you read the chapter on making your own jigs, you will learn that jig making is easy, fun and rewarding

JIGS AND MORE

Innovative anglers who were not afraid to try new ideas invented jig-fishing for salmon and steelhead. Today, I consider jig-fishing to be in its early phases. Not a year goes by without some creative angler finding a new twist to the technique.

JIG AND BAIT

For many years Great Lakes anglers have combined jigs with a variety of baits, including wax worms, spawn bags and whatever else they believe might tempt a steelhead to strike. Their success speaks for itself. Somewhat surprisingly, not many Northwest anglers have tried using bait-and-jig combinations. I can tell you that the dual attraction of bait and jig can be deadly.

I have used jig-and-prawn combinations for years on chum salmon. On occasion, when I have run out of bait, I have had to involuntarily test the relative effectiveness of the jig without the bait, as compared to the jig with the bait. The results are stunning. I can typically catch chums at twice the pace by adding a bit of prawn meat to my jig.

Serious steelheaders know that well-cured salmon eggs are arguably the very best way to catch steelhead. Many of us avoid eggs for a variety of personal reasons, but there is no denying their effectiveness. Recently, some steelheaders have begun tying up very small spawn bags, often as small as two or three eggs. They then slip the

The best jigs are tied with materials that undulate alluringly.

spawn bag onto the jig hook and have a lure that gets down fast, looks good and smells great.

The only limitation to what you can do with jigs and baits is your imagination. I have not yet tried crawdad tails, night crawlers, clams or sand shrimp, but I suspect they would all work.

In addition to adding natural baits, many anglers are adding scent to their jigs. I believe this is a huge advantage when fishing for salmon and can be of significant benefit when fishing for steelhead. The only disadvantage to baits or artificial attractants is their tendency to gum up marabou or other natural wiggly materials. If you want to use attractant, use care to keep them off the tail of the jig and carefully wash your jigs after each use.

JIG AND WIGGLE

On the West Coast we have been slow to add baits to our jigs, but we have been real innovators in adding a bit of wiggle to our jigs. After all, it was a natural marriage. Many top steelheaders were fishing with floats and pink worms before they made the switch to jigs. From there it was a natural progression to combining the two. Once anglers tried adding a bit of pink worm tail to their jigs, they saw their success rate shoot up. Then the real creative minds kicked in. Today, we see jigs combined with all sorts of plastic baits, from crappie lures to larger plastics designed for smallmouth bass. The one thing most of these combinations have is an alluring wiggle and good combination of colors.

JIG COLORS

There are few topics as controversial as deciding the proper color of lure to use. In broad, general terms you want to use subdued colors in gin-clear water and brighter colors in rivers where visibility is less than optimum. With that said, my all-time favorite color for steelhead, coho and chums in typical light and water conditions is fluorescent cerise. I would never leave home without some cerise jigs in my box. Yet many other top rods have other preferences. I recently posted a question on an Internet fishing bulletin board asking for opinions as to what was the best color jig for steelhead. At last count, I had eleven different answers. One thing I do know for certain is that color can be vitally important. I had that fact driven home years ago on the Salmon River.

The water was low and clear, and there were a ton of fish in the river. One slot in particular seemed to hold dozens of fish. I used my trusty cerise jig and landed six steelhead in short order. I gave the slot and my favorite jig to my friend Brad Knowles and he, too, hooked one fish after another. Eventually, we lost all my cerise jigs. The only other color I had was white with a hint of pink. Both Brad and I fished the white jig fruitlessly for a long time. It seemed as if the bite was over. Then while rummaging in my vest I found one last cerise jig. I tied it on and the bite was back on in full force. We continued to catch fish until dark.

In broad, general terms I suggest you arm yourself for steelhead with a selection of jigs in cerise, pink, red, white and black, or combination of those colors. For pink salmon, all you need is pink jigs. For coho, cerise is the top performer with red and white, blue-green and copper also performing well. For chums, cerise is tops, but many anglers swear by chartreuse as well. (Chartreuse is highly visible under many different water clarity and light conditions.) For chinook, pinks, reds, oranges, greens, and combinations of those will work well. The best advice I give on colors is to begin with the old standbys listed above and be flexible.

I believe that it is almost always beneficial to use jigs that have a combination of colors. The added contrast of two or more colors will draw more attention to your jig and will make it more appealing to many fish,

A jig combined with a bit of pink worm sometimes works wonders.

Jack Berryman battles a feisty Sauk River steelhead that fell for a cerise jig.

under a variety of conditions. One of the West Coast favorites, the Nightmare jig, uses a combination of black, red, and white to attract fish. The jig itself is quite simple and has no undulating materials to call a fish in, but many steelheaders swear by their Nightmare jigs and their success cannot be ignored. I suspect the combination of the three basic colors is the key to their success. Keep trying different colors until you find what the fish want that day. No one color will always produce, and what worked yesterday will not necessarily work today.

JIGS, COLORS AND DEPTH

What the fish perceive, and what we perceive, as color is a result of the refraction of light waves. Because water refracts light waves differently than air, the colors we see when we hold a jig in our hand are often very different than the color the fish will perceive 10 feet beneath the surface. When you take a red jig out of the box you see a bright, vibrant color that you may believe is irresistible to the fish. But as the jig sinks into the water column, what the fish see will often be simply a black shape. Each color reacts somewhat differently to depth, water color and clarity. Typically reds and oranges lose color most rapidly, while blues and greens retain more color at greater depths. Fluorescent colors react a bit differently than do non-fluorescent colors and, in general, will throw off more color at greater depths. Glow-in-the-dark colors will reflect at greater depth than all other colors.

For our purposes we need only know that a fish must be able to see the jig to strike it and that on occasion a jig can appear to be so bright that the fish will shy away from it. (Fish do not have eyelids and cannot rapidly constrict their pupils. The only way they can decrease or eliminate too much visual stimuli is to move away from the source of the stimulus.)

Most of us do not want to take the time to fully understand all the science behind underwater color refraction, but it is vital that we present a jig the fish can see and that our jig does not spook the fish. There have been entire books written on the subject of what fish see, and I recommend that you consider getting a copy of *What Fish See*, by Dr. Colin Kageyama, if you want to fully understand the subject. In general, you will want to begin your color selections by remembering these basic considerations:

If fishing in relatively clear water, at depths of less than eight feet, most colors will reflect well. Begin with pinks, reds, cerise and fluorescent colors in those shades. If fishing clear water under sunny conditions, switch to less-dynamic colors to avoid spooking fish.

As depth increases, and water clarity decreases, switch to fluorescent colors, as well as blues, greens, chartreuse, and fluorescent white.

In low-visibility conditions caused by muddy water, consider lures in black, gold plate and chartreuse.

In low-light conditions try gold plate, black and chartreuse.

You will immediately notice that many of the above-recommended colors are not readily available in today's jigs. That's all the more reason to give serious thought to making your own jigs to assure you have colors that are best for whatever conditions you find on the river.

Dave Vedder with a fat coho that fell for a Zzinger jig dropped through a bait ball near Campbell River, British Columbia.

SUMMARY

- Use a long rod if fishing with fixed floats.
- Always use the smallest float that will carry your terminal gear.
- Use monofilament on bait-casting reels and spun-fiber lines on spinning reels.
- Any weighting system will work as long as it properly weights your float and does not spook the fish.
- Jig size and color are the two most important considerations.

CHAPTER 6

CATCHING STEELHEAD IN RIVERS

IF YOU HAVE CAREFULLY READ THE preceding chapters on tackle selection, reading waters and why jigs work so well, you are ready to hit the river in search of steelhead. Because I know that I almost never read anything in order, I suspect you may not have done so either. Therefore, this chapter will cover a few things that have been discussed previously.

As you know, the majority of the water in any given river will have very few, or no, steelhead present. There is no sense wasting time flailing away at water the steelhead don't like. If you are not thoroughly familiar with reading water and don't understand where steelhead like to hold, this is a good time to go back and read the chapter on holding water. Assuming you know a likely spot to find steelhead, here is how to catch them on a jig.

PREPARATION

Approach the water as quietly as possible. If afoot, be stealthy, wear colors that blend in with the surroundings and walk slowly. If in a boat, do not run over the water you intend to fish and approach silently if at all possible. A steelhead that is comfortable and feels safe is not hard to catch. One that is scared is almost impossible to catch.

While river conditions, weather and many other variables make every day different, there are a few constants that are worth considering whenever possible. Steelhead will hold at the tail of a pool much more often than at the head, therefore, always try to be the first person to fish a good-looking tailout.

Before you get to the river you will have chosen your preferred rod and reel. If you are fishing smaller rivers from a boat and most casts will be less than 50 feet, you will have a spinning rod and reel rigged. Your terminal gear will consist of a small float that sits just right when coupled with the jig you have chosen and no additional weight.

If you are on foot and are fishing a large river where many casts will be more then 50 feet, you will have a 10- to 12-foot rod designed for a bait-casting or center-pin reel, and a float large enough to carry your weight and your jig. (It is best if you have tested your float before arriving at the river to be sure exactly how much weight it will carry properly. I use my hot tub and I know of others who use a deep sink to do their testing.)

Note that your float will have two color bands near the top. If fishing rough water, use just enough weight so that your float sits with the bottom edge of the lower color band right at water level. If fishing calmer water, use just enough weight for your float to sit with the water level at the bottom of the top color band.

Now it's time to tie on a jig. The choice of color is yours. On any given day one color will dramatically outfish another, but day in and day out, it's tough to beat pink, pink and white, or cerise. When in doubt, start with one of those colors. A later section on color selection will cover color choices based upon water depth and clarity.

Before walking or drifting up to the run, assemble your gear and adjust your float. Nick Amato taught me the value of being ready to fish when you get to the river. One morning on the Salmon River, he hooked two fish while I was rigging my gear. Of course, I might have been able to rig more rapidly if my hands weren't shaking with anticipation. Now I try to be ready to fish when I get to the river.

Approach the run, but come no closer than necessary to make a good cast and control your float and lure. Your first cast should be aimed to land at least ten feet upstream of the fish. In low, clear water you may need to increase that distance to avoid spooking the fish. Aim your cast to land between yourself and the fish. Meaning that if you are on the bank and the fish is 25 feet out from the bank, you want your jig to pass by the fish between your position and the fish's. This is especially true in low, clear water conditions. Your first goal is to avoid spooking the fish. If your float lands on the far side of where you expect the fish to be, lift your rod tip and pull the float toward you until it's on the line of drift you desire. If it lands too close to your position, either let it drift past the suspected lie or abort immediately and recast.

THE RIGHT DEPTH

Almost all old-time steelheaders are quick to tell you that steelhead spend most of their time in the river with their

A dream photo of a dream fish. This chrome summer run hit a jig on the run and then performed aerial displays that would have impressed the Blue Angels.

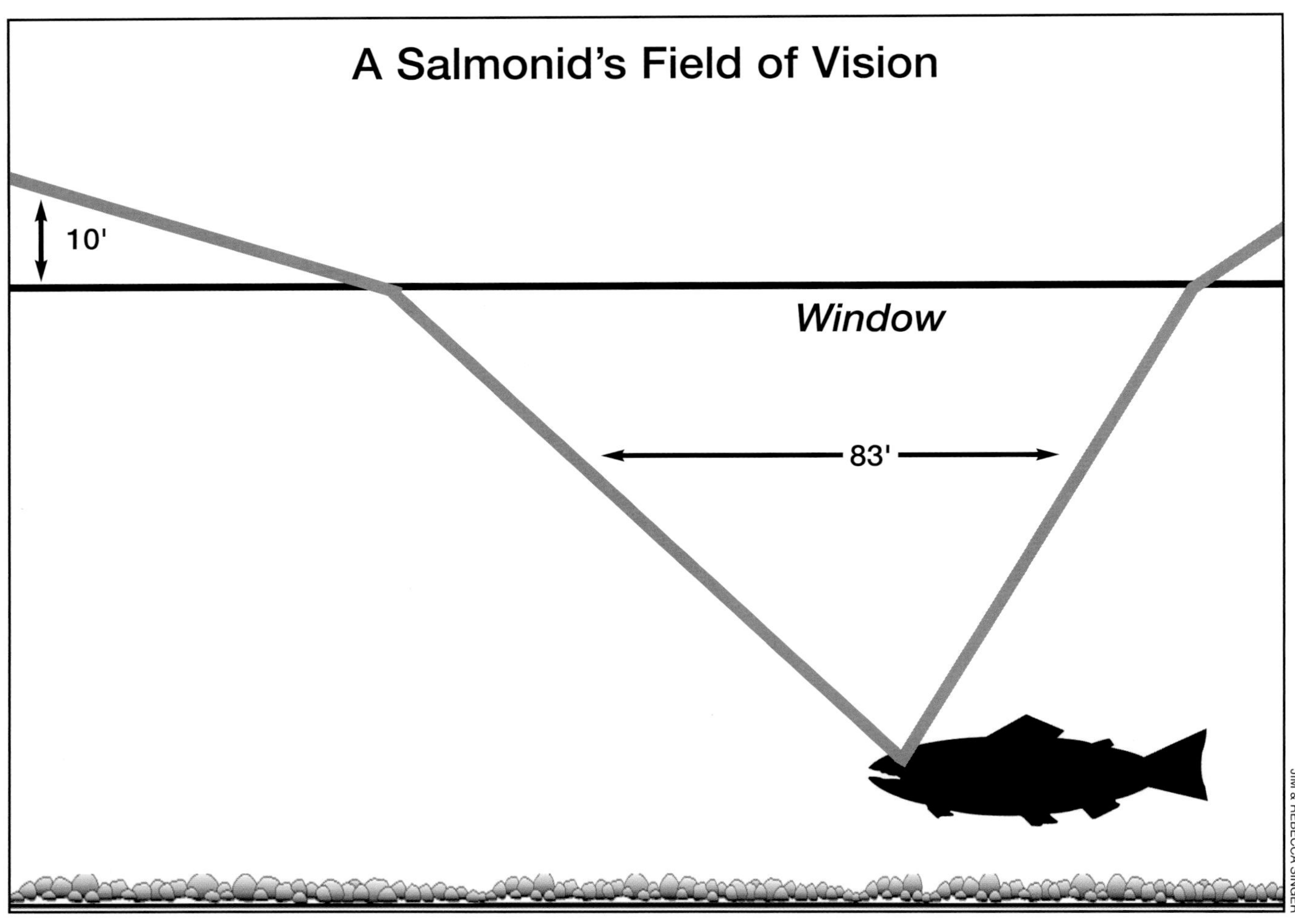

bellies near the bottom. And for many years, most of us fished with our gear tapping along on the bottom. I suspect that was mostly due to the fact that there is no other way to effectively fish the old-fashioned drift gear. Even many spoon and spinner fishermen aren t happy unless their lure occasionally taps bottom. (I should note here that my good friend and spoon-fishing guru, Bill Herzog, does not like to have his spoon ever touch bottom.)

As we began the switch to floats and jigs, many of us learned that steelhead will often come surprisingly long distances to smack a jig. Accordingly, many of us now fish our jigs well off the bottom. Summer-run fish in relatively warm water are not at all reluctant to come up three or more times to take a jig. Winter fish will usually not move so far, but they will come up for a well-presented jig.

Steelhead and salmon are designed to look to the side or up. They have no way to look down unless they turn their body parallel to the bottom to do so. Because a steelhead cannot look down, it makes very little sense to present your jig at a depth below that of the fish's eye.

I recommend adjusting your leader to allow the jig to pass above the fish by a minimum of one foot for winter fish and a maximum of five feet for summer fish. If you think the run you have chosen is eight feet deep, adjust your leader to present the jig about four feet off the bottom. Make a few casts at that depth, and then gradually lengthen your leader until your jig is passing over the lie, just above the bottom.

For less-active fish, adjust your leader to allow the jig to pass about three feet above the bottom. After a few casts at that depth, gradually lengthen your leader until your jig is fishing very near the bottom.

The most amazing proof of the importance of depth I ever saw happened on the Gold River in about 1994. My friend, Clint, and I were walking past the Campground Run on our way to another pool. An old German gentleman was the only person staying at the campground. We saw that he was working the spectacular run adjacent to the campground, so we decided to pass it by. Each day, for three days, we stopped to chat with him. He told us he had never caught a steelhead, but he knew there had to be fish in the run, and he wasn't leaving until he got one.

There were a lot of fish in the river. Clint and I were hooking more than twenty fish a day. We decided that there was no need to crowd in on the old guy's run. On our last day we once again stopped to chat with the gentleman. And again, he told us that he still had not hooked a fish. He said he had seen several steelhead rolling in the deep slot at the far side of the run, but he just couldn't get them to bite. Finally, Clint asked if the old man minded if he made a few casts. On his first cast Clint hooked a steelhead. On his second cast, he hooked another. And to my amazement, he hooked a third on his third cast. The old man was fishing in a slot that was about 12 feet deep, with only six feet of leader between his float and his bait. Every time he saw a steelhead roll, he would shorten his leader. These were lethargic winter-run fish holding in deep water. The only way to get a strike was to put the lure very near them. We showed the old fellow how to rig with a 10-foot leader and went on our way. When we returned, he was all smiles. He had finally hooked his first steelhead.

If your float tips downstream and jerks along, your leader is too long, and your jig is touching bottom. You should immediately abort the drift, reel in and shorten up your leader. Nothing will spook a fish quicker than hanging bottom near it, then yanking on the line until you break off. My good friend, Clint Derlago, calls jigs 'rock magnets,' and he's right. A jig dragging along the bottom will spook more fish than it will catch.

PRESENTATION IS EVERYTHING

Assuming your cast landed where you wanted, or you were able to move the float to the desired line of drift, you now need to carefully follow your gear downstream, As the float approaches you, reel in excess line. Your goal is to have no unnecessary line on the water, but to reel in carefully so as not to cause the float to be tugged in any way.

The perfect drift is one where the float moves downriver at exactly the same speed as the current. Your float should not be moving across the current, nor should it be moving slower or faster than the current in which it rests. (There is one exception to this rule that I will discuss later.)

I can think of nothing as important to success with jigs as the concept of a drag-free drift. Any time your float is doing anything other than drifting at the exact speed of the current, you are wasting your time. One reason the jig is so effective is that we can present it in a very natural manner. If your float is moving in perfect harmony with the river's currents, your jig will be doing the same.

Beautiful scenery is a big part of steelhead and salmon fishing.

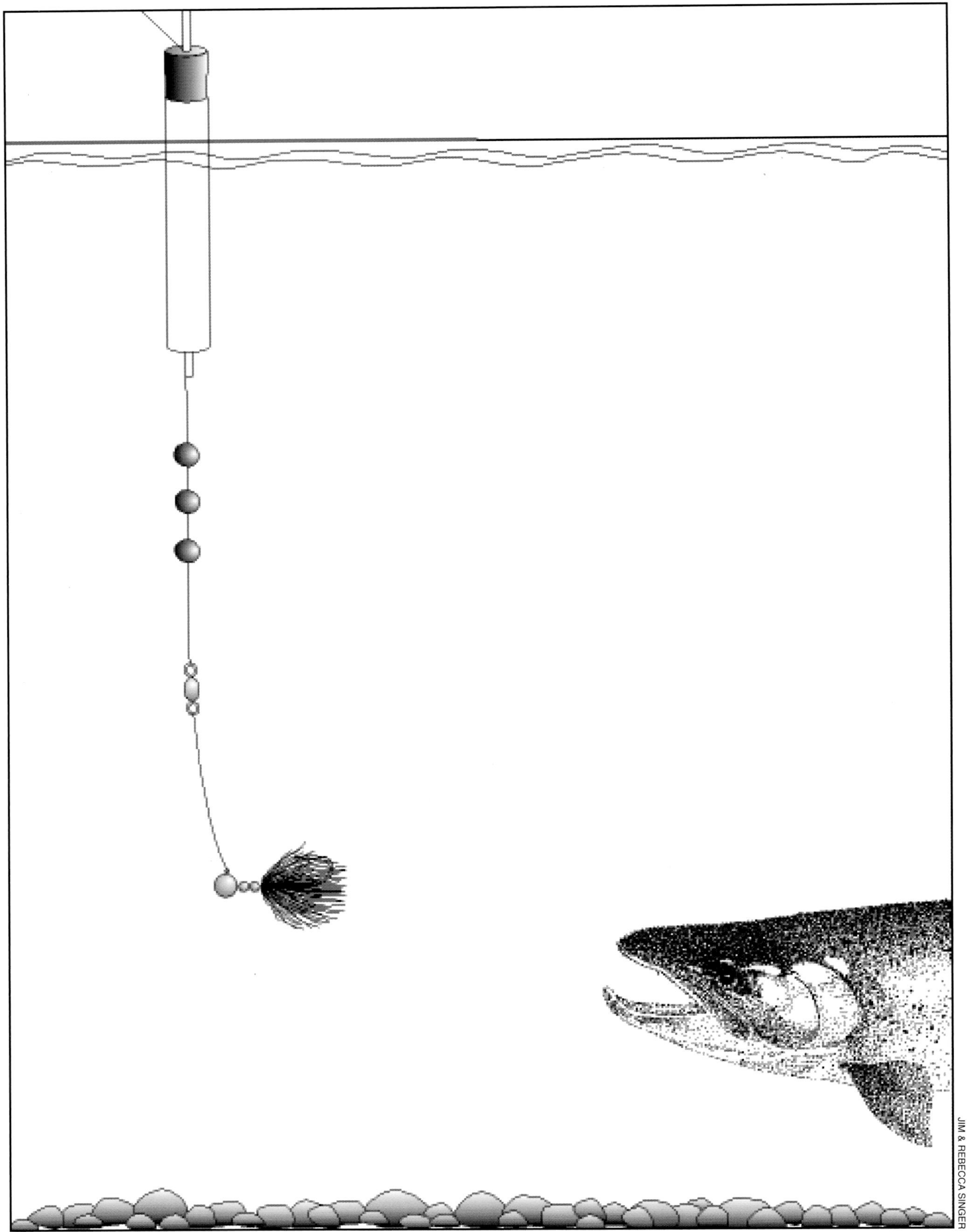

Your float must sit straight in the water to get a drag-free drift.

Steelhead are quite used to seeing things drift past them. Even in seemingly gin-clear waters, small bits of debris, insects, leaves and many other things are constantly drifting past the steelhead's lie. When a steelhead sees something coming at a strange speed or angle, it will immediately sense that something is not right. Occasionally, an unusual presentation will trigger an aggression strike, but more often than not a steelhead will not be interested in anything that seems to be acting unnaturally. If you have a drag-free drift, your float will be straight up and down in the water.

Fly-fishers know the key to success in fishing trout with a dry fly is to avoid any drag on the fly. In the case of dry flies, drag can be seen when a small V is formed in the surface film. That V is proof that the fly and the surface upon which it rests are not moving at exactly the same speed. With a float, the same visual signal is often present. If your float is making a V in the water, you do not have a drag-free drift. Likewise, if it is sitting at an unnatural angle, you do not have a drag-free drift.

The most common reason why we fail to achieve a drag-free drift is excess line on the water. In many instances the surface of the river is not flowing at a constant speed. Water behind an obstruction will be moving more slowly than water that is unimpeded and water that has just passed through a constriction will be moving more rapidly than water a few feet away. As a consequence, any excess line lying on the water between you and the float represents a chance for your float to begin drifting unnaturally. If your float is in a current seam that is moving at three knots, and there is a seam between you and the float moving at five knots, any excess line on the water will begin moving faster than the float and will ultimately drag your float both downstream and towards you. When that happens, you are no longer fishing effectively.

This Vedder River angler understands the importance of keeping his line off the water.

MENDING TO AVOID DRAG

An excess of line on the water between your rod tip and the float will almost invariably cause drag. The best way to avoid this is to use a rod long enough to allow you to keep all excess line off the water. But, on occasion, especially when you are making long casts, you will not be able to avoid having some line on the water. The solution is to mend your line. This is very easy. Imagine you are on the riverbank with the current running from your left to your right. You make a relatively long cast, hold your rod high to keep the line off the water, but even so, 20 feet of line is lying on the water. As your float and line move downstream, you can see that the current is pulling the excess line downstream faster than the float is moving. As a result, your float is being pulled downstream and toward the bank. To stop the drag, point the rod tip toward the water, reel in all excess line possible without putting any additional pressure on the float, then sweep the rod tip upward and upstream to flip the excess line back upstream. If you are not familiar with mending, you should go to a local river and practice before you head out after steelhead. With just a bit of practice you will be able to effortlessly flip excess line upstream. The perfect mend will cause the excess line to land upstream from your float

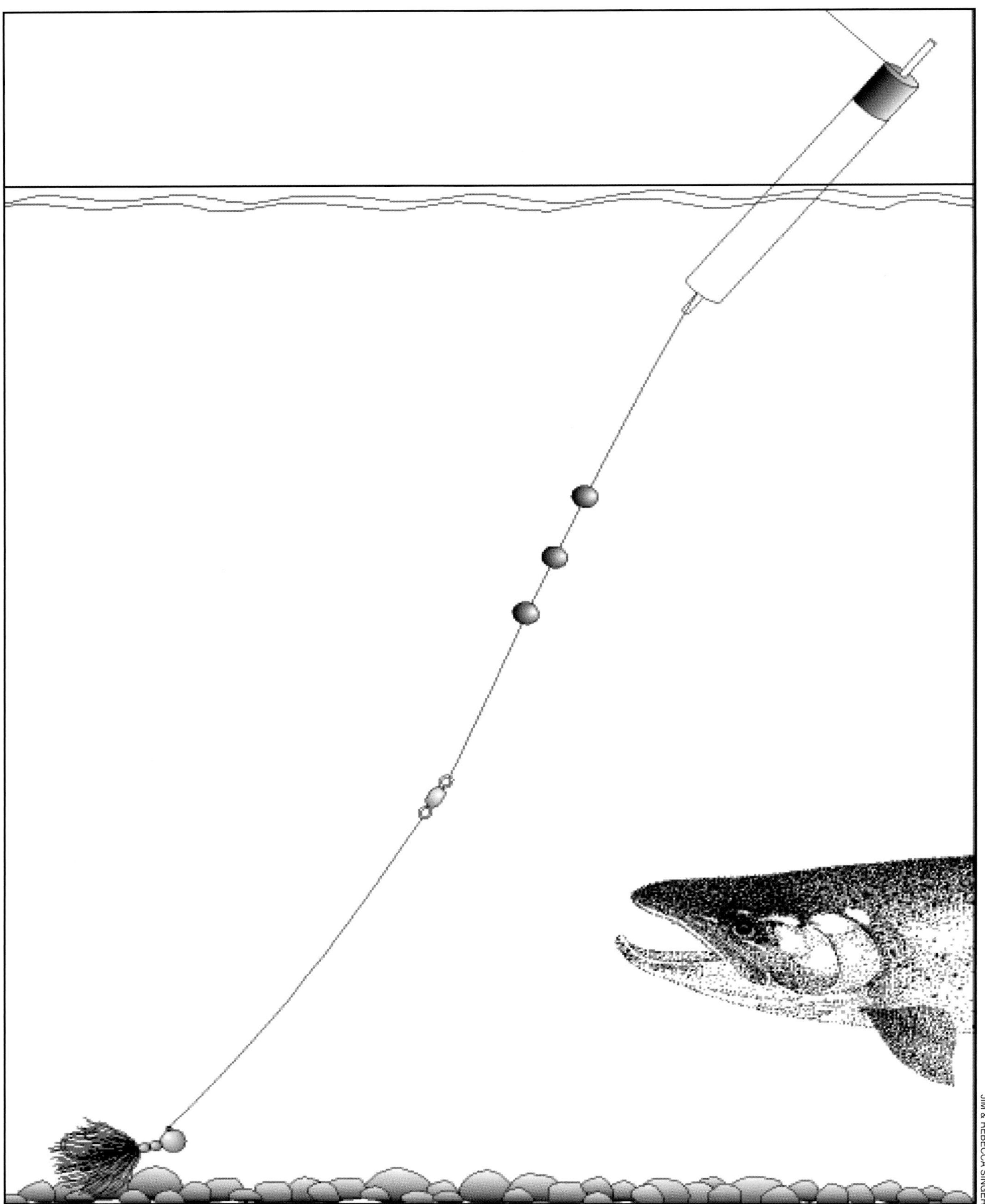

If your leader is too long the jig will drag on bottom and the float will tilt downriver.

and will not cause your float to jerk around as you mend. Like any technique, practice makes perfect.

Mending can be done easily with almost any line that floats. The new super braids mend very easily, as do most monofilaments. If you are using a monofilament, you may find that dressing the line with mucillen, fly floatant or anything that makes it float better will be an advantage. There are a few monofilaments on the market that tend to sink. Avoid these when fishing with a float and jig.

OTHER CAUSES OF DRAG

Another cause of drag is resistance to the line coming off the reel. As your float moves downstream of your position, you will need to let line come off the reel as smoothly as possible, to avoid placing any drag on the float. With a bait-casting reel, that's as simple as hitting the free-spool button, but a reel that is not in top operating condition may have a jerky spool which will cause an unnatural drag on your jig every time your spool hangs up. A similar problem occurs when you have a small bird's nest buried deeply beneath the line that is spooling out. I have had poor luck getting a drag-free drift with the new super braid line. I find that they tend to dig in on the spool and come off in a herky-jerky manner. Others swear by them. They do float well and are a breeze to mend.

With spinning reels, there should be no drag from line coming off the reel if the bail is open. But you do need some sort of control to keep the line from coming off the spool too fast. Most folks use a finger or their palm to very gently keep a bit of friction between the line and the spool. Until you master this feathering technique, you may have problems with occasional drag when you press a bit too hard on the spool.

Center-pin reels are the smoothest of all reels, which is one reason why many advanced float-fishers prefer them. A good-quality center-pin reel will feed line so smoothly that drag is seldom an issue.

Too much line between the float and the jig, allowing the jig to constantly bounce along on the bottom, causes the worst possible form of drag. Not only is this a very poor way to present a jig, it is a sure-fire recipe for a hang-up. You will lose far more opportunities to hook a steelhead with too long a leader than you will with one that is a bit too short.

NOW WE ARE FISHING

Once you have made that all-important first cast, you need to keep three things in mind. You need to be sure your float is moving downriver on the proper course. If you have cast a bit too far, it's an easy thing to simply lift the rod tip enough to drag the float into the correct position. If your cast was quite a bit too short, you need to bring it back and cast again. Next you need to watch the float to assure that you are getting that all-important drag-free drift. If your float jerks and tilts downstream, you are dragging bottom. Immediately reel in and shorten the distance between your float and the jig. If your float is being pulled to the side, or is making any type of V in the water, you have drag caused by failure to allow line to freely come off the reel, or too much line on the water. Either mend the line or move with the current to get that all-important drag-free drift. Lastly, you need to be very alert for a strike. More about that later, for now let's continue upriver, working various types of water.

A TYPICAL POOL

Most pools have three distinct parts: the head at the upstream end where the pool begins, the gut or middle section which is usually deep and relatively slower moving than the head, and the tailout where the pool shallows up and picks up speed before spilling into the next run.

If you are the first person to get to a pool, always begin at the tailout. Steelhead can be unpredictable, but the odds are the tailout will hold more fish, and more active fish, than any other part of the run. Often steelhead will stop and hold in tailouts to rest after moving through a section of rapids.

THE TAILOUT

In some ways, fishing tailouts can be challenging and in other ways quite easy. To fish a tailout effectively, you will need to begin by casting to positions near your feet and letting the float drift toward the tailout. As the float approaches the tailout you will need to hold back to force the float to pull your jig up in the water column. (Yes, this is an exception to the rule of a drag-free drift.) This is to avoid snagging bottom as the tailout shallows up. Repeat this sequence by making a series of casts, each one a bit farther away from you than the last. At some point, you will find that you cannot manage any significant drag-free drift before the fast current begins forcing the float back toward your position. This is not a problem. As the float begins pulling toward you, hold back on the line to cause the float and the jig under it to sweep across the tailout. Make the first sweep well above the bottom lip of

Soft water behind rocks provide resting areas for steelhead and salmon.

the tailout and make each successive cast a bit longer, so that the jig sweeps ever closer to the lip of the tailout. Often steelhead will be holding at the very bottom edge of the tailout.

If you get a strike when your jig is rapidly sweeping across a tailout, it will be a violent one. The fish will have to dash out and snatch the jig while the jig is moving rapidly. As always, watch your float for any sign of a strike, but also be aware that you may actually feel a strike before you see it. Because your line will be taut as it sweeps across a tailout, the float will be tilted back toward your position and there will be very little slack in your line. These strikes are the most exciting ones you will have. Often the rod tip will yank down suddenly and before you know it a chrome bullet is dancing downriver in the froth of the tailout. If you are not careful to let the fish take line as necessary, you will find yourself with a broken line and maybe a broken heart.

THE CENTER OF THE POOL

To fish the deeper and relatively slower water in the center, or "gut," of the run, you need to move to a position where you can easily cover all, or a portion of, the run. Begin making short casts to the positions nearest your feet. Keep a drag-free drift and watch your float like a hawk. If you see obvious fish-holding areas, like big boulders, slots, undercut banks or current seams, work those areas hard. Make as many as ten casts to the best-looking areas and thoroughly work your way across stream by making longer and longer casts.

In relatively slow water, such as we often find in the center of pools, strikes can be very subtle. Often the float will yank under hard. These are what my friend Brad Knowles, calls "ass cracking hits" and we all love them, but more often, the float will simply sink, almost as if you have too much weight on. Other times it will move across the current and sometimes it will actually pop up as if the

Nick Amato hooked this large steelhead in the center of a fishy-looking pool. It took three color changes to entice this big buck.

Clint Derlago fishing the middle of a spectacular run on the Gold River.

weight has been removed. (This happens when the fish has the jig in his mouth and swims toward the surface with it. The result is that weight is taken off the float, allowing it to rise up.) After you have watched your floats dance merrily down the river surface for a few hours, you will understand what types of movements are natural and which are unnatural. Any time your float does anything unnatural, strike, and strike hard. If it's a fish, your prompt hook-set may make the difference between a hit and a miss. If it's a snag, a quick hook-set may save you some tackle. As one of my old steelhead buddies likes to say, "jerk or be one."

On occasion, you will need to hold back the float just a bit to keep your jig moving at the same speed as the current at the bottom of the pool.

THE HEAD OF THE POOL

Often, steelhead will be tucked right up into the fast, shallow water at the head of a pool. Fish that are moving upriver in a hurry will often stop for a bit at the head of the pool before moving into the next run. Summer fish that need additional oxygen and the cover provided by choppy water will often hold at the head of a pool. To work the top end of a pool you need to estimate the depth of the water just below where the pool begins. Usually, the water just above the head of the pool will be relatively shallow, often only one to four feet deep. However, the depth just below the lip of the pool may be as deep as five to 10 feet. You need to adjust your jig so that it is fishing at the depth below the lip of the pool, not the depth of the riffle above the pool. This can be a bit tricky, as you will be casting

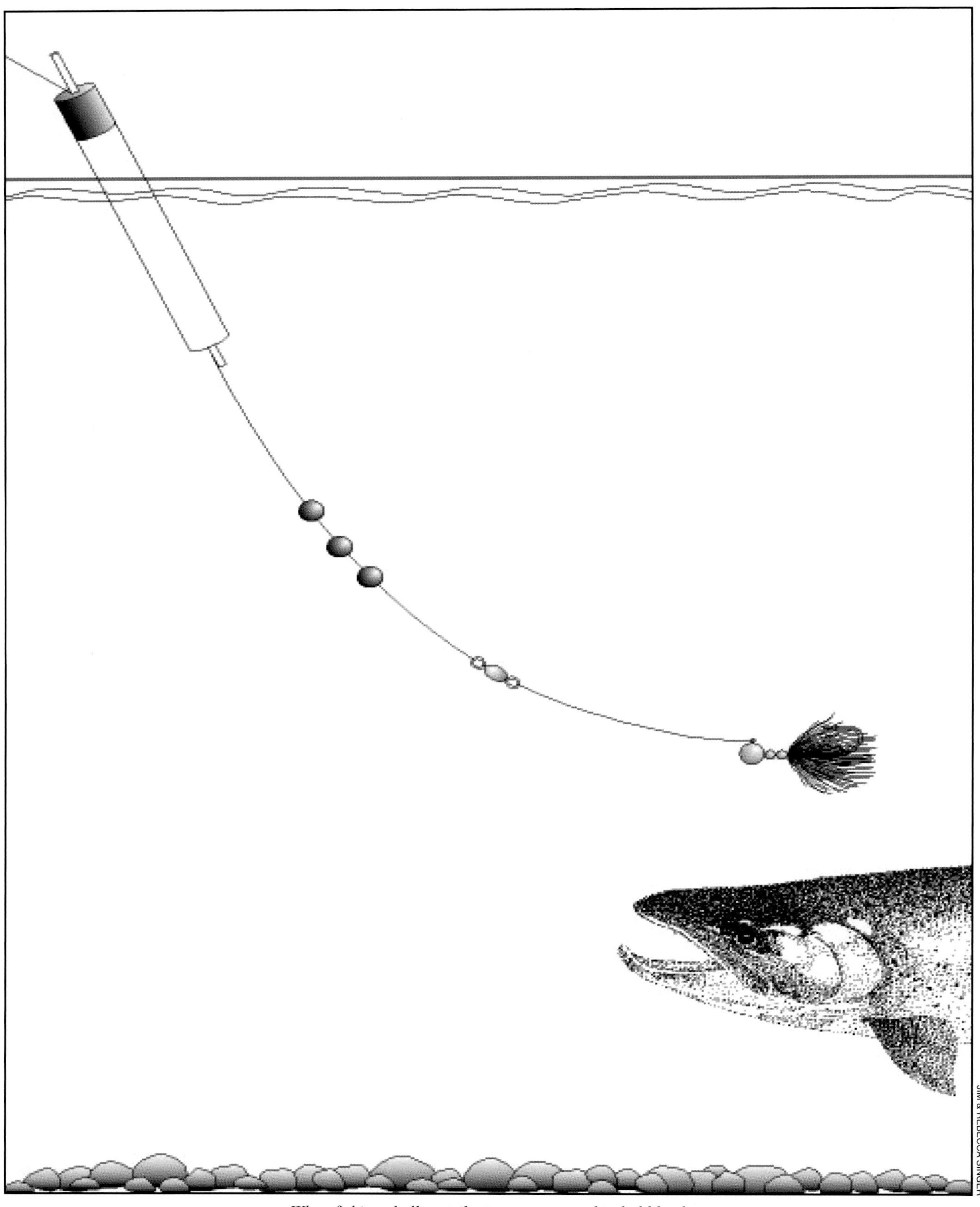

When fishing shallow tailouts you may need to hold back to keep your jig above the bottom.

into the shallow water above the pool with a leader that is designed to fish the deeper water in the pool.

When you cast a six-foot leader into three-foot water, it is inevitable that the jig will touch bottom. You need to be prepared for this. Be ready to lift your rod tip to keep the jig up off the bottom. Then drop the rod tip the moment the float enters the deeper water. This way your jig will be fishing at the correct depth almost the instant it reaches the fish-holding water.

As with the tailouts, and the gut of the run, you will want to fish the water closest to you first and gradually extend your casts until you have covered all good holding water. Many times the head of a pool will have a narrow chute feeding the pool. If that is the case, work the chute carefully then see if you can cast right to the edge of the pool at either side of the chute.

POCKET WATER

Many anglers mistakenly believe that jigs are not good pocket-water lures. That is just wrong. Because jigs sink into the strike zone so rapidly, they are ideal for those small slots and buckets behind boulders that we call pocket water. To fish these small pockets, you need to be hyper-alert, as well as ready and willing to lose tackle. Often, the water just above, below and on either side of the fish-holding pockets is shallow and fast. A perfect combination for eating tackle. You need to make accurate casts that land just upstream from the pocket.

If you miss the target by more than a few feet, you will need to abort the cast and try again. Many times, you will need to cast into water at the head of the pocket that is shallower than the pocket itself. To do this, you want to make your cast and immediately lift the rod tip to keep your jig off the bottom until the float sweeps into position. Then quickly drop the rod tip to let your jig swim through the pocket at the proper depth.

Most pockets are small enough that an undisturbed fish will take on the first or second cast. Nevertheless, if it's a prime-looking pocket, give it at least ten passes before moving on. If you just know there is a fish there, change colors and make another few passes before moving on.

Once, while fishing British Columbia's Chehalis River, I made about five casts to a fine-looking pocket, then moved on. After fruitlessly fishing downriver for a few hundred yards, I came back up and found another steelheader battling a 14-pound chrome buck in the pocket that I thought I had fished carefully. Steelheading requires hundreds of small decisions every day. You will often hook more fish by working lots of water with only a few casts to each pocket. Other times, you will need to

Many anglers pass up pocket water, which is an excellent reason why you need to fish it.

The float and jig are a perfect combination for slow-moving water.

carefully work fish holding waters with a variety of sizes and colors to finally draw a strike.

STILLWATER FLOAT FISHING

Many steelheaders never have the chance to fish steelhead in still, or very nearly still, water, but the opportunity does arise. Perhaps the most heavily fished steelhead water in the world, the confluence of Washington's Blue Creek and the Cowlitz River, is one such place. The mouth of the Methow River, where it empties into the Columbia, is another. In these locales and many others, the float-and-jig combination offers such an obvious advantage that even die-hard drift fishers have abandoned traditional bottom-bouncing gear in favor of the float and jig.

One of my favorite stillwater experiences came on the Olympic Peninsula's Salmon River. It was one of those banner days when everything came together just right. The river was high and dropping, the fish were in and we had been hooking a ton of steelhead. Near the end of the day, we came to a long, deep pool that seemed to be more like a lake than a river. At that time I had not fished jigs in still water and wasn't sure what to do. I adjusted my float to put the jig about eight feet deep and let it drift ever so slowly toward the tailout. As I was watching my float, frankly, with little hope of any action, another angler came up to the pool. Float-and-jig-fishing was still quite new then and he had never seen a dink float. He asked me how they worked and I told him. I had hooked nine steelhead so far that day. He then said he could see how they might be effective in fast water, but didn't see much use for them in deep pools like the one we were fishing. At that moment my float yanked under and I set the hook on my tenth steelhead of the day. Now we both knew that a float and jig could be a great choice for fishing still water.

Many stillwater steelheading areas feature deep water and heavy concentrations of steelhead that may be holding well above the bottom. This is an ideal situation for the jig-fishing steelheader. Still water that is less than eight feet deep may be fished well with traditional fixed floats, however, these quiet waters often run from 10 to 40 feet deep. These conditions call for a slip float.

Still waters are best fished with light lines, small floats and lures that provide a strong, visual stimuli without the benefit of movement provided by strong current flows. Light lines are necessary, because clear water and slow-moving lures give steelhead lots of opportunities to examine our offering.

Small floats are used because there is no need for the buoyancy required to keep the float visible in choppy water. Another reason for small floats is their increased sensitivity. Stillwater steelhead often nibble delicately, so delicately that the bite is barely discernible. Tiny floats telegraph these tiny bites.

Almost every size and color of jig has taken steelhead in still water, but the best success usually comes with small jigs in pale colors or black. The best stillwater jig can provide an alluring wiggle even when at rest. Marabou, rabbit fur and schlappen all work well in quiet waters.

Many stillwater float-fishers use an outfit something like this: an 8- to 9-foot rod designed for 6- to 8-pound-test line, a spinning reel filled with 6-pound line, a small slip float and a 1/16- to 1/8-ounce marabou jig. Favorite colors are pale pink, pink and white, and black and purple. Many experts use a small piece of shrimp meat on the hook of their jig to add flavor and scent.

Still waters have little in the way of seams, riffles, or other surface markers to provide a hint as to what is beneath, but you can still do a bit of detective work to find the lay of the pool. As with moving water, use your float as a depth indicator. Simply keep lengthening the distance from float to lure until you know how deep the area is.

Steelhead in deep, still water are not always oriented with the bottom as is common in flowing water. One day you may find the fish quite near the bottom of a twenty-foot-deep pool, the next day they may be near the bottom at the six-foot depth, and yet another day they may be suspended ten feet deep in twenty feet of water. Trial and error, keen observation of others, and sharing of information with other anglers will help you learn at what depth fish are holding.

Even in relatively still water, subtle currents and wind move your float. It's a good idea to keep your reel in free-spool while applying slight tension on the spool with your thumb, then let your float slowly slip downstream, or as the wind or current dictates. If circumstances require an upstream cast, slowly retrieve line as the wind and current push the float back towards you. It is imperative that you keep all slack out of the line and watch your float like a hawk.

Stillwater pools are often major staging areas for steelhead. This group of steelheaders is fishing a nearly still pool on the Quatse River.

Tom Gordon with a beautiful, wild summer steelhead that was taken during the middle of a sunny day in the lower Deschutes River. Jig-fishing is a great way to cover hard-to-reach spots.

Stillwater steelhead will often take the lure very gently. Many times the pick-up is signaled by a slight lift of the float as the fish releases the tension on the line by mouthing the jig, other times the only indication is a slight jiggling of your float. You must learn to strike very quickly when these tentative strikes occur. If you wait too long, the fish will drop the bait. If the float is lifting up, jiggling or, best of all, is fully under water—strike!

If you miss the chance to strike, don't despair. Stillwater steelhead often return to your jig as long as a bit of bait remains. This time be ready and strike the instant the float does anything that says "fish." Stillwater steelhead are affected by changes in barometric pressure, much like bass. When a cold front passes through, with a dropping barometer, they go off the bite or become very tentative biters. Fishing is usually best in stable weather.

WHEN YOU KNOW WHERE THE FISH ARE

As you approach the pool or run you have chosen, stop a few feet short of the pool and watch. Look carefully for areas where steelhead will want to hold, behind boulders, against banks and in boulder gardens. Carefully scan the entire run with polarized glasses. With practice, you will learn to spot steelhead. One trick is to forget about seeing what looks like an entire fish. Instead, look for a shape that seems fishy, a shadow that doesn't look like others, a fin or a tail. Occasionally, you will see a steelhead roll on the surface. Don't be fooled by the top-water action. Sure there is a steelhead there, but it will be holding with its belly near the gravel by the time you can begin fishing over it.

If you see a steelhead that is undisturbed, naturally you will want to go after that fish. Begin by making a cast that lands your float at least ten feet upstream from the fish's lie and a bit toward your position. Remember that if you can see the fish, it's likely it can see you. Stay low, move slowly and try to make a delicate cast that lands with little splash. If your first cast does not get a strike, try casts that progressively work closer to the fish. (Closer in terms of your position on the bank and the fish's position in mid river.) Never make a cast that lands less than ten feet from the lie. If you have presented your jig in a natural drift, and you are sure the steelhead saw it without spooking, it's time to try a different color and perhaps a different size. Keep working the fish until you have shown it several colors and sizes of jigs. Many times I have seen a fish ignore cast after cast, only to turn and slam a different-colored jig. Don't be quick to leave. After all, many days you spend most of the day trying to find a fish. Never leave fish to find fish!

THE STRIKE

As I discussed earlier, steelhead take a jig for a variety of reasons ranging from anger to curiosity. As a result, the strike may vary from a tiny nibble to a slam-dunk.

One of the great joys of steelhead fishing is visiting the spectacular places where they live.

Steve Henry with his first jig-caught winter steelhead. Steve has been an avid steelhead fisherman all his life. He commented, "This is too easy," as he made another cast.

Naturally, the aggressive takes will yank your float right under. There will be no mistaking that type of take, but often the float will telegraph a strike in subtle ways. Top jig anglers know that any strange or unnatural movement of the float may signal a strike.

Watch your float very carefully, especially on the first cast into a suspected lie. There are two reasons why the first cast is most important. For one, many times an aggressive steelhead will take a jig the first time it sees it. The second reason is you want to know exactly how your float behaves in the run you are fishing. For example, you may note that your float dips under in a particularly heavy current seam and then bounces right back up. If so, it's obvious that you do not want to set the hook every time your float dips down in that spot. Conversely, if you note that your float is doing anything that it didn't do in the run on previous casts, you need to strike and strike fast.

In addition to the more obvious strike indications such as a quick yank under the surface, your float may signal strikes in many less obvious ways. For instance, on occasion the float may suddenly begin floating higher than it has previously. Strike! The sudden raising of a float is a sure sign a steelhead has picked up the jig and has lifted it a bit higher than it was originally drifting. That will cause your float to rise up and should cause your arm to come back hard. Another sign of a strike, that some anglers miss, is when the float begins moving across the current. This happens when a fish picks up the jig and moves at roughly the same depth as the jig, but moves across the river. If you see your float move in any direction other than the current flow, strike.

When you do strike, be sure to do so with enthusiasm. My old friend, Bill Davis, said the best way to strike is to try to hit yourself in the pants with your rod tip. My friend, Clint, sets the hook so hard I can hear his rod whistle through the air. Far more fish are missed by wussy hook-sets than by overly aggressive hook-sets. Steelhead will seldom hold an unscented jig for more than a few seconds. Once you suspect a fish has your jig in his mouth, it's time to hit hard and fast. Even when fishing with light line, if your rod is appropriately matched to the line in use, you will seldom break your line on a hook-set.

If you want to get a better feel for how strong your line is, try tying it to the bumper of your car then practice setting the hook. You will be surprised how forgiving today's rods are. Next try standing a few feet away from the bumper and slowly raise your rod tip until the line breaks. Again you will be amazed at how much pressure even six-pound-test line can take.

FISH WITH CONFIDENCE, FISH HARD

Nothing about steelheading is easy. I suspect we wouldn't love it so much if it were. One key to success is to keep on casting. Some days the fish seem almost too easy to hook, but on others, one fish may be all you can hope for. Too many times to recount, I have hooked a fish after many others had given up. In British Columbia a group of my friends have formed the last cast club. The rules are simple. All you need to do to gain admittance is announce your last cast then hook a fish on that cast. To date there are only a few members, but they all know that the last cast may be the one that makes their day a success. In the

Confidence is the key to success!

1800s an English angler offered this advice to his fellow fishing fanatics:

> *"Should you be of delicate temperament and be wading in the month of February when it may chance to freeze very hard, pull down your stockings and examine your legs. Should they be black or even purple it might perhaps be as well to get on dry land; but if they are only rubicund you may continue to enjoy the water."*

If those Old English anglers could put up with such conditions, surely we, in our fancy waders, can put in the time it takes to make that one last cast.

My father took up steelhead fishing after he turned 65. By the time he was 85 he was a top rod. Several times I saw him walk into a run, where several other anglers were unsuccessfully working the water, and promptly hook a steelhead. Many old-timers who fished the Humptulips in the 60s held him in awe. It almost seemed is if he had some sort of fish magic. I asked him one day what his secret was and he told me, "Every cast I make, I know I am about to hook a fish." That was some of the best advice I ever got, and it will stand you in good stead too. If you believe you are about to hook-up, you will fish with confidence and you will be ready for the strike when it comes. Nothing is more important than fishing with confidence.

SUMMARY

- Approach a suspected lie slowly and carefully.
- Cast only where you expect to find a fish.
- Fish the tailouts first.
- Avoid drag at all costs.
- Set the hook hard any time the float does anything unusual.
- Stay Optimistic – Fish with Confidence – Fish Hard.

7
CHAPTER

JIG-FISHING FOR SALMON IN RIVERS

TODAY, JIGS ARE COMMONLY USED BY many top steelheaders, but those who angle for salmon in our rivers have been slower to take up jigs. That is unfortunate because I am firmly convinced that properly fished jigs will take as many, or more, coho, pinks and chums than

Most steelhead jigs will work for salmon, but coho and chinook often prefer a larger and flashier jig than do steelhead.

Coho simply love jigs. If you put a jig in front of an undisturbed coho you have a high chance of a hook-up.

any other method. Chinook salmon can be taken on jigs and under the right conditions, jigs can be deadly for chinook. The only salmon that seems unwilling to take a jig is the sockeye. Perhaps one day someone will find techniques that consistently draw strikes from sockeye, but as of now I know of no such techniques.

Because each species of salmon requires slightly different techniques, I have divided this chapter into separate sections for each species. Sockeye, due to their stubborn refusal to take a jig, have been purposely omitted. To avoid any favoritism in the presentation of my salmon-jig-fishing information, I had planned to present the species in alphabetical order. (But the truth is, coho are by far my favorite.)

COHO

Like so many of the salmon family, coho go by several names. In Alaska they are "silvers." In Canada they go by coho and in the U.S. they answer to either appellation. Coho are my favorite salmon because they are willing biters, they fight like hell and, while I admit that beauty is most certainly in the eye of the beholder, I find coho to be

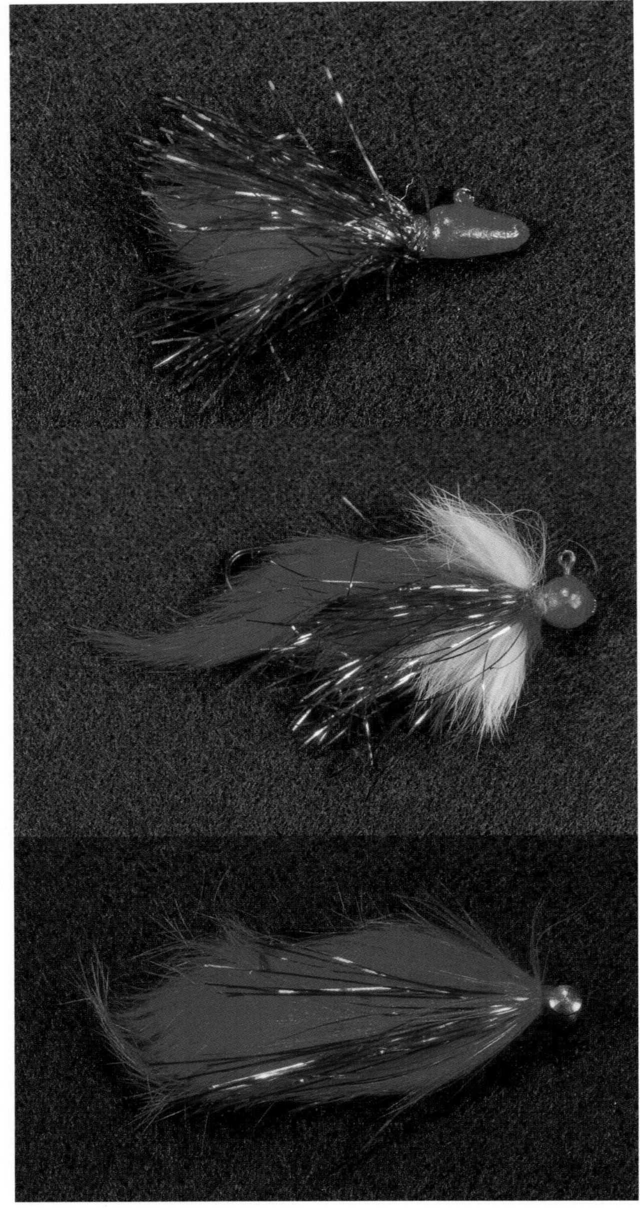

Three coho/chinook/sockeye jigs designed by Gordon Gracy of Forks, Washington.

the most beautiful of our salmon. There is a very good reason why coho are often called silvers. A fresh coho, with long-tailed sea lice on it, is as bright as a mirror. Often, when several species are in the river at the same time, you can tell it's a coho simply by the flash of its chrome sides when it strikes. If the flash isn't clue enough, a sizzling run, followed by several cartwheeling leaps, should confirm your suspicions.

One of the best-kept secrets of the 90s was the fact that coho simply love jigs. Olympic Peninsula guide Bob Kratzer was one of the first to consistently take river coho on jigs with no float. He began using a homemade jig consisting of a 1/4-ounce jig head with a pink plastic hoochie slipped onto the jig. Bob was able to keep his secret for several years, but eventually, many other guides learned how easy it could be to take coho on jigs.

River coho tend to hold in slow-moving water. Often you will find them in deep, slow runs, in back channels and side sloughs. If there are large numbers of coho present, you will often see them finning on the surface or even rolling and jumping. Coho typically jump and reenter the water gracefully. These slow backwaters are the perfect place to fish jigs. Because you want to impart an up-and-down movement on the jig, it's important that you fish in slow-moving water. It is nearly impossible to give a jig the proper action in rapidly-moving water.

Coho are very willing jig-biters, but to draw a strike you need to forget all you know about jig-fishing for steelhead and think in a very different way. The first thing you need to do is take off the float. Yes, coho can be tempted to take a jig that is presented under a float, but you will take many more if you get rid of the float.

When fishing jigs for coho, you need to impart an up-and-down jigging motion to your lure. This is best done with a jig tied directly to your main line. You need not bother with any additional weights or with a float. The key to success is to impart an erratic motion to your jig. Make your cast and let the jig settle to near the bottom. Then lift your rod tip about a foot and immediately drop the tip back down. As the jig falls, reel in the slack created by the drop. Your goal is to let the jig fall freely, but keep slack to a minimum. Try to keep your jig down in the strike zone, while maintaining a lift-and-drop pattern. Do not reel in while lifting your rod tip, as that will make your jig swim to the top. It takes practice to be able to make the jig hop along with an up-and-down motion. Many anglers raise their rod tip too high, which makes the jig come up too far and usually results in fishing too shallow. Try to visualize your jig hopping along, near the bottom, with quick one-foot hops that are immediately followed by a rapid drop-back near the bottom.

Most strikes will come as the jig is dropping back toward the bottom. When you start to lift the rod tip you will feel pressure. Sometimes the strike is savage, and there is no doubt you have angered a coho. Other times all you will feel is slight pressure or the sensation that the jig is suddenly heavy. Set the hook hard and fast. Coho will

Coho tend to go for bright colors and lots of flash.

not hold a jig for long, so you must stay alert for even the slightest bit of unusual pressure.

Keep jigging until your jig is all the way back to you. Many times, coho will follow a jig for a long distance before striking. When they see that it looks like it's escaping they will sometimes inhale it. Other times, you will see a swirl as they take off back to the bottom. Sometimes their tail will splash you as they flee.

I find that coho like jigs in the 1/8- to 3/8-ounce size range. Favorite colors are cerise, pink, red, green, blue and copper. Feel free to experiment with various combinations of these colors. A favorite combination of mine is blue and green.

It is child's play to make your own coho jigs. Just buy an assortment of jig heads with a strong wire hook. I prefer Gamakatsu's hooks. They make a variety of jig head shapes and sizes, and their hooks are both sharp and strong. Place the hook in a vise and start tying-in your favorite colors of synthetic materials such as Flashabou. For jig heads in the 1/8-ounce range, I like the dressing materials to be approximately 1.5 to 2 inches long. For larger jig heads make the dressing materials slightly longer. Avoid the temptation to pile on too much material. Sparsely tied jigs will usually shimmy and wiggle best.

Another really easy way to make your own coho jig is to buy packages of small hoochies. Just slip the jig head into the hoochie and force the eye through the hoochie. Sometimes you will need to make a tiny slit, near the head of the hoochie for the eye of the hook to pass through. Major tackle shops will carry a variety of sizes and colors of hoochies. Stick with the ones in the 1.5- to 2.5-inch lengths. Coho seem to avoid large jigs.

That's really all there is to making your own coho jigs. There are many good jigs on the market that will do the job. Just remember to look for jigs with strong hooks in the 1/6- to 3/8-ounce size and select colors previously recommended.

CHINOOK

Only recently have I become aware that some anglers are doing quite well targeting chinook salmon with jigs. Because I had little personal experience fishing chinook with jigs, I did some research to learn who might best teach me. I soon learned that Mark Anderson, manufacturer

Chums are suckers for cerise jigs. I know of no other method that is more effective when targeting chums.

First Bite Jig manufacturer Mark Anderson landed this jig-caught Wilson River chinook.

of First Bite Jigs, was well known as an expert on the subject. I was able to talk Mark into taking me chinook fishing with him on Oregon's Wilson River. The day we fished together was far from ideal. The river was low and very few fresh fish were moving in. Nonetheless, in about half a day we hooked two chinook and a coho. While one day on the river does not qualify me as an expert, I spent a good deal of time interviewing Mark and others who are using jigs for chinook. This is what they told me.

WHERE AND HOW

Mark said one reason he began actively targeting chinook with a jig is the fact that he catches quite a few incidental chinook while fishing for summer steelhead. The best presentation for chinook is similar to that used for steelhead. A drag-free drift is as important as putting the jig right in the face of the chinook. River chinook are notoriously finicky biters. In most cases they will not move far to take a lure or bait. As a result, when fishing chinook, it is important that you do your best to figure out exactly where in the run the fish should be, and then repeatedly present your jig to every position that may hold fish.

When targeting river chinook, look for water flowing at about the pace of a slow walk. Most chinook you hook will be in water that is from 6-15 feet deep. The slower water gives the fish just enough time to see the jig and decide if they want to take it. With chinook, most of the takes are out of curiosity.

When fishing water that is rising, look for fish to be on the move and focus on water that will intersect their path. tailouts are perfect places to intercept moving fish. When fishing tailouts, run your jig a little shallower and try to keep it at a slower pace.

When fishing low, clear water you need to try running your jig right off the bottom in deeper holes around 8-15 feet deep. Resting fish tend to hang close to the bottom, and they like substrate that has a rocky bottom with boulders from the size of a fist to the size of a basketball.

BEST JIGS

Chinook usually prefer large lures. Mark and others who regularly target chinook use jigs in the 1/4-ounce to

JERRY FERRO

The Quad by First Bite Jigs.

3/8-ounce range in bright colors such as cerise, hot pink, blood red and hot orange. As with other salmon, multi-colored jigs are often a good bet. Artificial materials such as Krystal Flash and Flashabou are great additions. Matching the Krystal Flash to the colors of the feathers makes a pleasing jig. Many of the best chinook jigs have three or more colors. One of Mark's best-selling jigs is called "The Quad," and is made up of four different shades of pink and cerise.

Chinook jigs must have big strong hooks. If you simply tie on one of your favorite steelhead jigs to go after chinook, you may hook a few, but you lose many. Ideal jig hooks are extra strong, large gap, Gamakatsus or Owners, in sizes 2/0 to 4/0. Thin-wire hooks simply will not do the job.

Mark and many others often add scent to their chinook jigs. I think this is a great idea, as chinook are notorious for their attraction to certain scents. Many anglers tip their jigs with sand shrimp or raw prawns. While not too many use roe, I believe the addition of a small spawn bag is a great idea. Scented oils are also often used. Shrimp scent and anise are favorites of the experts. When using any scent, be sure to try to keep jig feathers free of the scent and wash your jigs after the day is done.

TACKLE

For leader material, I recommend something in the 20- to 25-pound-test range. Chinook are not particularly line shy and anything lighter will simply result in too many lost fish.

For their main line, many anglers prefer 30-pound Power Pro braided line. It floats which is a big help for mending line, it casts well and the small diameter allows the use of reels that do not have a huge line capacity. Others still favor monofilament for its forgiving qualities and low cost.

For your reel, the choice is largely one of personal preference. I see many anglers in Oregon using spinning reels; while most in Washington and British Columbia prefer bait-casters. What is important is that you choose a reel that has a strong drag system and will hold at least 120 yards of 20-pound-test line.

Naturally, your rod must match whatever style reel you choose. An ideal rod should be rated for 15- to 25-pound-test line and needs to balance well with whatever reel you use. Choose a rod with a fast tip to get solid hookups on the typical tentative bites of chinook.

MARK ANDERSON

A beautiful chinook jig by First Bite Jigs.

CHUMS

Not too many years ago, almost no one fished for chums. They were considered scrap fish not worthy of our efforts. When I was a pre-teen, I fished in the huge shipyard derby in Bremerton, Washington. Just after daylight, I hooked a really strong fish that battled valiantly. After a long fight my dad netted my fish, a sixteen-pound chum. Imagine my disappointment when I was later told my fish was not going to be considered for a prize because the derby officials considered chums to be scrap fish. Now we know that chums can be great battlers, and if taken while still

Chums simply love a cerise jig.

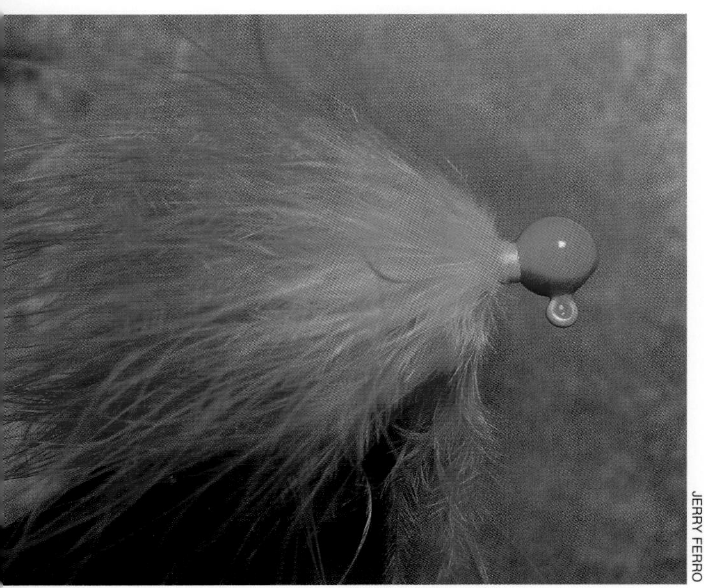
JERRY FERRO

Chinook jig.

fresh with bright-orange flesh, they are excellent smoked or on the barbeque. Only recently have we discovered that chums love jigs.

Bill Herzog was the first person I saw take a chum on a jig. We were fishing over a huge school of chums in water so clear we could see fish all over the run. We had tried the usual assortment of chartreuse lures and yarn with absolutely no luck. As Bill likes to say, "We didn't even get a hard stare." Finally, Bill rigged up a dink float and a 1/4-ounce cerise jig. He began catching chums like magic. We soon learned two really important things. Chums love a dead-drifted jig under a float, and cerise will usually outfish any other color. Time and again, I have consistently outfished guys who stubbornly stick to their beloved chartreuse lures and yarn. While I freely admit that all salmon can change their color preference from day to day and even hour to hour, I remain convinced that a cerise jig will almost always take chums.

Pinks will readily slam a small pink jig. For best success retrieve your jig in small twitches.

My all-time favorite chum rig is a dink float, enough added weight to properly cock the float and a cerise jig. Because chums like a dead-drift, the float is the perfect way to present your jig. Fish it as you would for steelhead, with care to always get a drag-free drift.

Chums tend to hold in the water column, sometimes well above the bottom. Adjust your float to put the jig about two feet above the bottom. If that doesn't work, shorten it up a bit more. Several times I have seen guys put in frustrating days without a fish, simply because they were fishing too deep.

Chums tend to move upriver rapidly until they reach the general area in which they intend to spawn. This is typically in the lower third of the river system. Often, old stale chums that are nearly ready to spawn will be found very near the edge of the river. These are not desirable fish and should be avoided. But in many cases, out in the strong current, you will find chums that are still in fine shape and these fish are usually good biters.

I find that chums can go off the bite for no apparent reason. When they get lockjaw, there is little that will tempt them to strike. One trick that almost always seems to work is to add a small piece of shrimp meat to your jig. I buy Tiger Prawns at the supermarket and carry them in a small Zip-lock bag in a pocket of my vest. (If you should forget and leave these in your vest for a few days, you will soon smell the error of your ways!) You do not need much shrimp meat on your jig to improve your hook-up ratio. A three-inch-long prawn will make at least ten baits. You may find it convenient to cut up your shrimp before heading to the river. To fish them, simply slip a small piece of shrimp up past the barb and you are ready to go. Some anglers cure their prawns in the same way they do salmon eggs. This makes attractive bait that works well. I usually don't bother, as chums seem to like the uncured baits quite well. Sand-shrimp tails will also bring you strikes. I tend to avoid them, as they are more expensive than prawns and they are much more fragile.

Like all other salmon, chums don't always follow the rules. If the old stand-by cerise jig and shrimp does not work, don't be afraid to experiment. I have taken chums on jigs in pink, red, black, orange and chartreuse. On occasion, I find that going to a smaller jig will bring success when the fish are finicky. If nothing seems to be working, take a break, watch the river flow by for a bit, and try again later. Chums can go on the bite as if someone threw a switch. Many times I have gone hours without a strike when chums were all around. Then as if someone rang the dinner bell, I hook one fish after another until my arms tire out.

Even big rivers can be effectively fished with a float and jig.

If you do decide to target chums, be sure to bring heavy gear. Chums are, pound for pound, the strongest of our salmon. A twenty-pound chum in fast water can be a serious challenge. I recommend a rod rated for 10- to 20-pound-test line, 17-pound-test monofilament and jigs with extra-strong hooks.

PINKS

jig-fishing for pinks has very nearly replaced all the old standbys, such as small, thin-bladed spoons and the larger, pink-colored spoons. The reason for this is simple, pink salmon are absolute suckers for a twitching jig. More than ten years ago, Nick Amato and I were fishing for summer-run steelhead in a small British Columbia river.

On my second cast, I caught a nice summer-run but after that, we just couldn't find another biter. As we worked our way downriver, we began noticing a few fresh pink salmon in each run. The farther downriver we went, the more pinks we saw. Nick decided that the steelhead weren't going to cooperate, so he suggested we try to find where the stream we were fishing entered the Fraser. After a bit of back-road exploration and some bushwhacking we arrived at the mouth or the river. Nick's guess was right, there were thousands of chrome-bright pinks stacked up at the river mouth. Nick had been fishing steelhead with a float and a small pink jig, so he decided to try the same outfit on the pinks. They were not impressed. Ever the experimenter, Nick decided to take off the float and try giving his jig some action. The results were amazing. Nick hooked fish after fish on his small pink jig, tied directly to the main line. It didn't take me long to follow suit, and I too began jigging pinks. We hooked so many pinks there was no way to keep count. Certainly we caught and released at least 50 pinks that afternoon. To this day, my favorite pink salmon lure is a 1/8-ounce pink jig tied directly to the main line.

Like coho, pinks tend to hold in slow water, back eddies and sloughs. However, traveling fish can be found in faster water. To work jigs well, you need to avoid areas of heavy current flow.

When fishing pinks with jigs, you must give the jig an up-and-down jigging motion. This is best done with a jig tied directly to your main line. You can catch pinks with a jig under a float, but you will catch more if you take the float off and work your jig. The key to success is to give your jig an up-and-down hopping motion. After your cast, let the jig settle to near the bottom, then lift your rod tip about a foot and immediately drop the tip back down. As the jig falls, reel in the slack created by the drop. You want to let the jig fall freely, but at the same time, keep slack to a minimum. Try to keep your jig down in the strike zone while maintaining a lift-and-drop pattern. Don't reel in while lifting your rod tip. That will cause your jig to come to the top. It takes practice to be able to make the jig hop along with an up-and-down motion. Many anglers raise their rod tip too high, which makes the jig come up too far and usually results in fishing too shallow. Try to visualize your jig hopping along, near the bottom with quick one-foot hops that are immediately followed by a rapid drop back near the bottom.

Most strikes will come as the jig is dropping back toward the bottom. When you start to lift the rod tip, you will feel pressure. Sometimes the strike is savage and there is no doubt you have angered a pink. Other times all you will feel is slight pressure or the sensation that the jig is suddenly heavy. Set the hook hard and fast. Salmon will not hold a jig for long, so you must stay alert for even the slightest bit of unusual pressure.

Keep jigging until your jig is all the way back to your rod tip. Often pinks will follow a jig for a long distance before striking. When they see it heading to the top, they will sometimes inhale it. Other times you will see a swirl as they take off back to the bottom. Either way, it's a real thrill.

As far as colors and sizes go, pink and small is about all you need to know. Pink salmon simply love anything pink-colored. My favorite pink-salmon jigs are 1/8-ounce pink marabou or rabbit fur. On the other hand, you can make a deadly pink-salmon jig by simply slipping a small pink hoochie over a 1/8-ounce jig head. I have taken pinks on relatively large jigs, every year thousands are taken on Buzz Bombs and other relatively large lures, but for consistent success with pinks, stick with 1/8-ounce jigs.

Many folks disdain pinks. I think that's a shame. I think a fresh pink salmon, with long-tailed sea lice still attached, is a real battler. Unfortunately, too many people fish them with tackle designed for steelhead or larger salmon. If you outfit yourself with a spinning rod designed for 4- to 8-pound-test line, the diminutive pink salmon will give you a serious scrap.

SUMMARY

- Use a float and a drag free-drift for chums and chinook.
- Use a jigging motion for coho and pinks.
- Try tipping your jig with prawn meat or sand-shrimp tails when targeting chums, coho, and chinook.

8
CHAPTER

JIGGING FOR SALMON IN SALT WATER

I BELIEVE THAT NO OTHER METHOD OF fishing salmon in salt water is as exciting or as productive as jigging. There are only two keys to success when jigging salmon in salt water. One is to find the fish and the other is to match the hatch. Because most salmon are voracious feeders while in salt water, the key to finding the salmon is to find the bait they prey upon. Typically, that means finding a bait ball, regardless of whether the bait is herring, candlefish, sardines or anchovies.

Every experienced salmon angler has watched in awe as baitfish shatter the surface, pursued by feeding salmon. Many of us have found excellent action by working our favorite bait or lure around the edges of such action. But all too often we have been frustrated to find that not all bait balls have salmon in pursuit, and those that do seem to disappear like fog on a sunny day. Typically, we work the area for a few minutes, and then go back to our trolling or mooching. A much better approach is to pull your gear and go in search of another bait ball. A famous bank robber was once asked why he continued to rob banks. His answer was, "Because that's where the money is." It's really that simple with salmon. Most of the time they will be found where the bait is.

THE JIGS

Top jigs include Zzingers, Point Wilson Darts, Buzz Bombs, Crippled Herrings and Dungeness Stingers. Favorite colors include white, green and white, blue and white, and chrome. When it comes to jig selection, there are as many theories as there are fishermen. I know that most of the jigs on the market will work under the right circumstances, but to be consistently successful you need to know what size bait the fish are targeting and then select your jig accordingly. For salmon feeding on herring, a full-bodied jig like the Crippled Herring or Zzinger is ideal. If the fish are targeting candlefish, you will want to switch to a long, thin jig. As far as colors go, you need to begin your search with white, white and blue or white and green. These all reflect light much like a baitfish does. If you are jigging in deep water, consider switching to a fluorescent white jig.

Your choice of color is largely a matter of personal preference. The inventor of one of our most popular jigs fished his new lure with no paint at all and caught a ton of salmon on it. Later in his life, when he used lures from his inventory, he tended to go with gray jigs that were about the color of the unpainted lead. Where and how you fish a jig can be much more important than what color you use. Remember that all colors fade to black at depth. Reds lose color fastest, while greens and blues retain color at greater depths. If you are fishing at depths of more than 50 feet I suggest white jigs and fluorescent-colored jigs. Even though color fades at depth, fish will still key on jigs at great depths. I once caught canary rockfish on a jig at depths of more than 400 feet.

Doug Wilson's joy is obvious as he shows off a 36-pound chinook that slammed his jig.

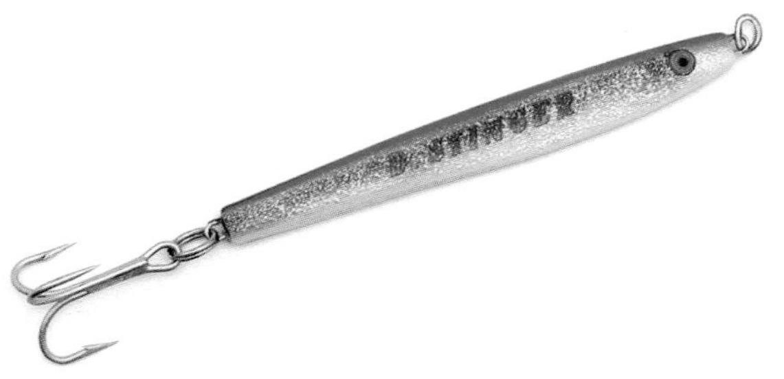

When salmon are feeding on candlefish, a long slender jig like the Deep Stinger will match the hatch.

One important variable that cannot be overemphasized is the importance of razor-sharp hooks. Salmon will only hold a jig for a few seconds, so it's imperative that you have sticky-sharp hooks and a lightning-quick hook-set. Many jigs come with treble hooks, which do a poor job of penetration, but an excellent job of tangling in the net and snagging bottom. I replace the trebles on all my jigs with 2/0 Gamakatsu siwash hooks.

Countless trophy-class chinook have fallen for a jig that fluttered past them as they were marauding a bait ball.

JIGGING RODS

Many jiggers make the mistake of using rods that are too long and too soft. I often see jiggers using soft action mooching rods up to ten feet long. These rods waste a lot of energy and do not allow for a solid hook-set. Every time you lift a long rod to make another jigging motion, much of your energy goes into bending the rod. The jig moves only after the rod bends. Because you often need a rapid hook-set, and to avoid wasted energy, I prefer a relatively short, stiff rod. My favorite is the Lamiglas Puget jigger, which is seven feet, six inches long and rated for 2- to 6-ounce lures. Any rod with similar attributes will do the job.

REELS

Any good-quality reel will work for saltwater jigging, but I prefer a bait-caster with a high-speed retrieve. Often, you will feel a small tick as the jig drops, when that happens you need to immediately begin reeling up as fast as possible. A reel with a fast retrieve works best for that. I do not care for spinning reels when jigging in the salt. It takes too much time to flip the bail over before beginning a retrieve after a strike. In addition, I believe it is easier to control the drop of your jig with a bait-caster.

LINE

Jigging for salmon in salt water requires a line that is sensitive and has little stretch. This is where the new super braids shine. These lines are almost perfect for jigging, but they do have some special considerations. Because the super braids are so limp and flexible, it is very easy to wrap the line around your rod tip when actively jigging. This can be a major irritant, but you will learn soon enough to keep your jigging action smooth to avoid the problem. The other consideration with using braided lines is that they have absolutely no stretch. If you set the hook hard on a shallow fish, while using a stiff rod, something will give. It's easy to break rods, tear out hooks and even break line when using the super braids. Even so, I believe they are the way to go when jigging. You just need to use them a few times to get the feel for how they work best.

STALKING YOUR QUARRY

The key to successfully finding bait balls, and the salmon that so often accompany them, is to cover a lot of water, fast. This requires a good depth finder, properly mounted, and a willingness to burn fuel until you find the fish. You

Doug Field, the inventor of the Zzinger jig, with proof that jigs can be deadly.

The Luhr-Jensen Crippled herring is a proven salmon slayer.

must lay down your fishing tackle and focus on the search. This is best done by cruising as fast as possible without losing the signal from your depth finder. If you have a properly mounted depth finder you should be able to cruise at fifteen to twenty knots while receiving an excellent signal.

With one eye on the depth finder, and the other on the water, cruise until you find a school of bait. Don't worry about cruising too fast to see the bait. The bait schools you are looking for are at least 10 feet in diameter. On occasion, you will find bait schools that are 100s of feet across and up to 40 feet thick. A typical school of baitfish will appear on the screen as a haystack-shape, but there are no hard and fast rules here. Sometimes the bait will be in a tight ball—a sure sign they are threatened by predators. Other times, they will be scattered over an area larger than a football field. No matter what shape you see, you need to stop and investigate.

USE YOUR FISH FINDER

Your most important weapon for jigging salmon is your depth finder. An ideal system for high-speed salmon stalking features a unit operating in the 196- to 200-kilohertz range with a 16- to 20-degree transducer. You do not need an expensive unit to do the job. If fact, the old-fashioned flasher units work quite well for showing bait schools and salmon. You need to be sure that your depth finder is properly mounted. Most depth finders will record accurately at speeds of up to 40 knots, if properly mounted. This lets you cover a lot of water while looking for the next bait ball.

For best results, mount your transducer inside the hull to avoid false signals created by water turbulence. You may have to try several locations to find the one that works best on your boat. It's surprising how many schools of bait do not have salmon following them. A top-quality depth finder will usually be able to discriminate between baitfish and salmon. On some depth finders the baitfish will show as small fish symbols and the salmon as much larger looking fish. On paper graph machines and many other depth finders the mass of bait will turn the screen black, but below the black mass you will often see large V shapes, which are usually salmon.

Once you become experienced at interpreting what your depth finder is revealing, you will quickly be able to decide if salmon are present. If you do not see salmon under the bait, try slowly cruising around the school. Pay particular attention to the down-current side of the school. Strong currents often sweep baitfish along. When that happens the school may form a shape like a comet. There will be a ball-shaped main body with a tapering tail comprised of straggling baitfish. Often, the salmon will follow along, picking off stragglers near the end of the tail. If you are certain no salmon are present, it's time to start searching again. If you see salmon on the fish finder, it's time to drop them a line.

This is what you are looking for, a good-sized bait ball with salmon underneath. This is usually almost a sure thing!

LET IT FALL

The best way to tempt a salmon to strike an artificial lure is to present it in a falling, fluttering or rotating manner. Nothing does this better than lead jigs. Underwater video, shot by Charlie White, shows us exactly what happens when a pack of salmon attack a mass of bait. The salmon rush into the school with jaws snapping like steel traps. Each snap of the salmon's jaws brings instant death to several baitfish. Often, several others are injured. Once a salmon has made three or four passes through the school, they rest and swallow the baitfish still in their mouth. Often, the resting salmon will see injured fish twisting and slowly falling toward the bottom. No matter how

This estuary coho pounced on a jig that was cast just ahead of where it had last jumped.

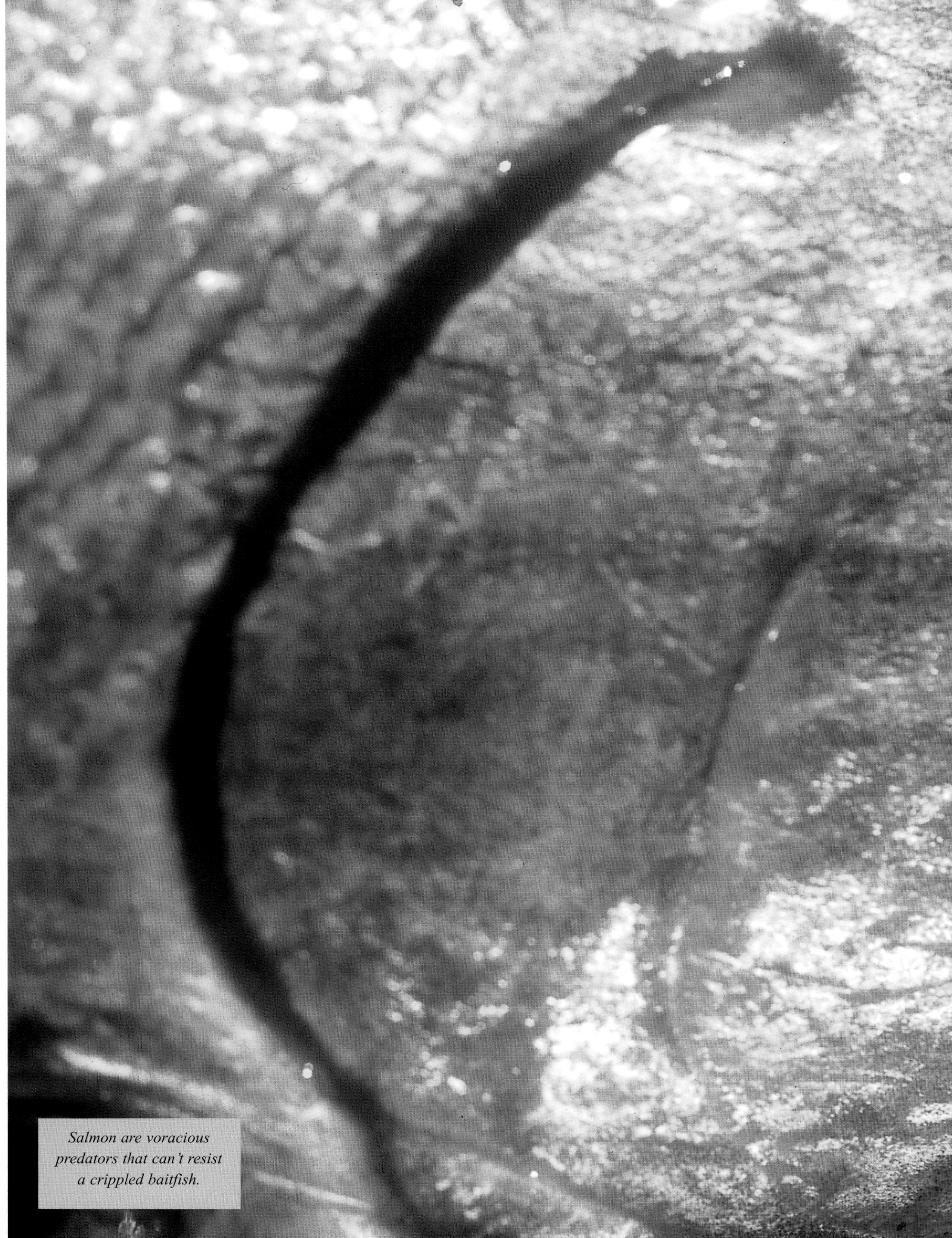

Salmon are voracious predators that can't resist a crippled baitfish.

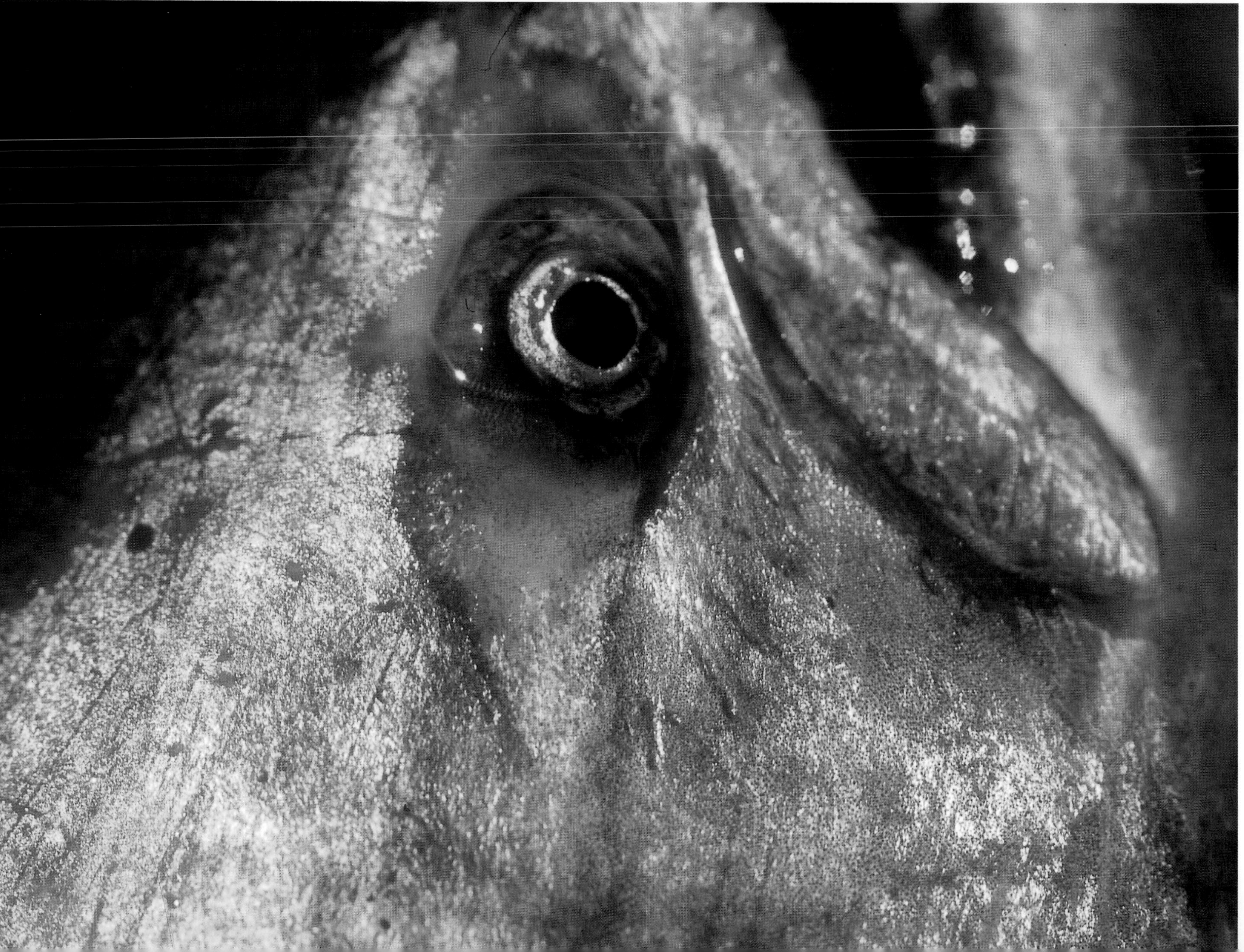

Chinook are suckers for a properly presented jig.

satiated the salmon are they cannot resist a crippled baitfish fluttering past. The salmon suddenly turns, flares its gills and inhales the helpless baitfish.

To trick the salmon into believing your jig is a wounded baitfish, select a jig that is the approximate size and color of the baitfish that are present. This is what I mean by matching the hatch. Tie on your jig and drop it through the bait to the depth where the salmon are holding.

It is important that you fish your jig at, or slightly above, the level of the salmon. Your depth finder will tell you how deep the salmon are, but you need a way to tell how far your lure has fallen. One good way to do that is to use a level-wind reel and to count the number of times the line passes back and forth across the reel. For example, the Abu-Garcia model 5000 releases about five feet of line with every pass across the spool. Using that information, you can estimate that it will take about seven passes for your jig to reach a depth of 35 feet. Naturally, every reel is different. You should take the time to measure how much line your reel lets out in one complete pass.

Once your jig is near the depth you want, simply lift the rod tip slowly and drop it back rapidly. It is best to let the jig free-fall while keeping in touch with the jig. In other words, as the jig drops, try to let if fall freely, but try also to avoid any excess slack. The best possible action is one that does not interfere with the jig's fluttering action, but has such little slack that you instantly know when a fish has stopped the jig's fall.

Another great technique is to free-spool line while maintaining a slight pressure on the spool with your thumb to avoid backlashes. Strikes invariably come as the jig is falling. Many expert jig-anglers never use the traditional lift-and-drop technique. Instead, they simply let the jig fall until it is well beneath the fish, then they reel in as fast as possible until the jig is in sight and repeat the process again.

A slack line is by far the most common indicator that you have a strike. Often, a striking salmon will dash toward the surface to intercept a falling jig. His momentum will keep him moving toward the surface for several seconds after he snatches the jig. When that happens, your line will go slack. This is no time for indecision. Rapidly reel up until the line becomes taut, then set the hook hard. If hitting bottom caused the slack, your fast hook-set may save you a hang up. If the slack was caused by a strike, you need to get a hook-set before the fish can spit out the jig.

If you know you are in 200 feet of water and that your jig is only 50 feet down, there can be no doubt that any slack you notice is caused by a salmon stopping the jig. If you have been observant, you will notice the pick-up almost instantly. A quick hook-set is called for. If you have been wool gathering a bit when you notice the slack line, you may need to reel in a few feet of slack before you set the hook

KEEP ON MOVING

Top rods such as British Columbia's, Doug Field, inventor of the Zzinger jig, seldom make more than five unsuccessful drops before moving on. Doug doesn't believe in wasting time. "If I am certain there are salmon down there, I will make six or seven drops. Then I will lower my Zzinger to a position a few feet above where I think the fish are and make a half-dozen lifts and drops. If that doesn't work, I speed-reel my Zzinger to the surface, then drop it back to the same depth. I will do this four or five times before I leave a bait ball. Some days, when there isn't much bait around, I may hardly drop a jig all day. But I know that if there's no bait, no one will be catching much anyway. Other times, when there was lots of bait, I have limited in less than an hour. My best bait patch ever had so many big chinook under it that I was able to limit my boat of five anglers with salmon ranging from 15 to 28 pounds. We had a double-header on our first drop and five on at once before we were through."

ESTUARY COHO

When coho stack up in bays in front of the river of their destination they can be extremely hard to hook. One of the greatest frustrations a salmon angler can endure is watching coho jumping all around you as they ignore every trick in your arsenal. The only way I have found to consistently hook estuary coho is with a cast jig. The technique, while not always successful, is surprisingly easy. Simply sit with your rod ready to cast and watch for a jumping or rolling fish. If you can see which direction the fish is headed, make a cast that lands your jig about 10 feet in front of the fish. Let the jig drop about six feet and begin jigging as you reel in slack. Lift the rod tip to bring the jig up in the water column, then drop the tip to let the jig fall. Reel in some slack and repeat. Most strikes will come on the first or second jigging motion, but don't give up on the cast until you can see the jig. Often, coho will follow the jig right to the boat and slam it as it nears the surface for the final time.

If you do not get a strike, reel in and wait until you see another fish to cast to. This works quite well for coho and occasionally works on chums as well.

SUMMARY

- The key to success in the salt is finding bait or leaping salmon.
- Make only a few drops on each school of bait. If fish are present, you will get a hook-up almost immediately.
- Choose a jig that is roughly the same size and color as the bait salmon feed on.
- Have a rod rigged and ready to cast in front of leaping coho.

CONCLUSION

"The first night we stayed at Fort Boise. I lay on the bank of the river, where I could scarcely sleep for the Indians who sang all night. This is their practice when they are gambling. The salmon also kept up a great noise jumping and splashing about in the water"

—Joseph Williams, emigrant, 1841, via wagon train.

I KNOW THAT IF YOU FOLLOW THE advice in this book, you will be able to hook more steelhead and salmon than ever before. My reason for writing the book is to give anglers a better way to enjoy the sport that we all love. But I am concerned that a few who read this will use these techniques to the detriment of our wild steelhead and salmon.

In most enlightened states and provinces, wild steelhead are protected from those who would kill them for the dinner table. Unfortunately, my home state is not so enlightened. I am embarrassed that Washington's regulators recently bowed to pressure from Indian tribes and local politicians to reintroduce catch-and-kill fishing for steelhead in a handful of Olympic Peninsula rivers. Yet, we, the governed, in many cases have principles that go beyond the petty politics of the regulators. Fortunately, the majority of steelheaders understand that wild steelhead are simply too rare and too important to end up on a dinner plate.

The catch-and-release ethic has become so ingrained amongst steelheaders that few would kill a wild fish even when the law still allows it. But as I watch our wild-salmon runs deteriorate in almost all parts of the West Coast, I have begun to realize that the catch-and-release ethic must be extended to most runs of wild salmon as well.

Because our salmon know no boundaries, wild, sometimes endangered, fish are often found intermingled with abundant hatchery fish. If a conscientious angler wants to do all they can to protect our wild salmon, we must immediately take the initiative to release almost all wild salmon hooked in the ocean and many of those found in our rivers, as well.

Too many times I have seen our fisheries' managers set bag limits and season on wild fish smugly telling us the runs are strong. Yet, repeatedly these same runs diminish and often become endangered. We cannot rely on our fisheries managers to be stewards of our wild fish. Their seemingly endless stream of failures proves only that they

Brad Knowles works a spectacular pool on the Chehalis River.

can, and often do, manage our wild fish into oblivion. In defense of our fisheries' managers, I understand that most are dedicated, hard-working anglers who choose their life careers, at least in part, because of a love of fish. Their failures are almost always the result of political pressures that come from the many special-interest groups whose interests are diametrically opposed to good stewardship of our natural treasures.

There is no doubt that, in most instances, the collapse of wild-salmon runs has been caused by factors other than sport fishing. The damage done by dams, clear-cuts, urban sprawl, commercial nets, pesticides and a host of other forms of human greed and ignorance have clearly been the prime cause of the collapse of many wild steelhead and salmon stocks. But that does not diminish the harm we can do by killing wild fish that have survived the gauntlet of obstacles we place in their path, only to be killed by fishermen after they enter their natal rivers.

I fully acknowledge that in some rivers wild stocks are strong enough to allow sport harvest. In those cases, when we are absolutely certain that our consumption of a few fish will do no harm, we should feel no guilt about taking our limit. But even then, there is no need to fill our freezers simply because the law allows it. Too many times I have seen sport fishermen brag they had a freezer full of fish and that they were trying hard to find someone to give their excess fish to. Many times the fish are tossed out the next spring to make room for the next season's catch. I believe this is simply a form of ego gratification. The thinking seems to go something like this, "If I have salmon to give to all the neighbors, I must be a great fisherman." In my mind, the great fisherman is the one who understands the intrinsic value of wild salmon, and whose strong sense of conservation dictates the need to release most wild salmon caught.

Fortunately, jigs are a near-perfect tool for the catch-and-release angler. Seldom will you find a fish with a jig so far down its throat that release is a problem. Most often you will find that the fish has been hooked in the center of the top jaw, a place that has no major blood vessels. If you take the step of voluntarily pinching your barbs, even when not required by law, you will be able to successfully release almost every fish you catch.

I absolutely hate the often-used phrase, "I threw it back." Unfortunately, I have seen salmon and steelhead literally thrown back into the water. I have even seen idiots kick fish back in the water. Please handle any fish to be released with the utmost care. Understand that the fish you release may be vital to the survival of that river's wild population. Whenever possible, keep the fish in the water. Unless you have a strong desire for a photo, simply reach down with long-nosed pliers and tug the hook from its lip. If the fish is exhausted, release it in quiet water where it can regain its strength without having to battle strong currents. Recent research has shown that it is not helpful to push the fish back and forth in the water. Simply hold it steady in slow current until it voluntarily swims away. I love it when a fish takes off with enough enthusiasm to splash water all over my face!

If a photo is desired, try to think of how you can get your picture without doing any more harm to the fish. Keep the fish under water where it can breathe until the cameraman is all set to shoot. If possible, keep the fish at least partially submerged. If it is legal to lift the fish out of the water, do so as gently as possible. Remember the fish is near exhaustion, and that it cannot breathe when out of the water. Think how you would feel if you were submerged after running as hard as you could until you could run no more. I freely admit that many times in the past I did not follow these suggested rules and for that I am sorry, but past errors do not preclude learning from our mistakes and growing as we mature.

When releasing a fish, we get the joy of knowing we won a battle of wits and skill. We get to make physical contact with one of nature's most amazing creatures, and we get the satisfaction of knowing the fish we release will spawn progeny that we, our children and our grandchildren may catch another time.

While I vacillate between optimism and gloom over the future of our wild fish, I do know that today's anglers are much more concerned with our heritage than were our predecessors, who simply couldn't fathom how we could ever lose such abundant resources as passenger pigeons, buffalo and wild salmon. Now we know that without our stewardship, the runs that greeted the first settlers can, and will, disappear forever.

Jigs are deadly when fishing cold water.

GREAT BOOKS ON SALMON & STEELHEAD FISHING

STEELHEAD DRIFT FISHING
with Bill Herzog and Nick Amato

Bill Herzog and Nick Amato will show you how to catch one of the world's favorite game fish. Not one, but two native winter steelhead pushing the 20-pound mark are hooked and released!

This tape will teach you everything you need to know to experience the thrill of hooking giant sea-run rainbow trout.

Subjects covered include: Seasons, range and types; reading water and decoding rivers; terminal gear and rigging; techniques for steelhead drift fishing; natural baits; and the tools—rods, reels, lines and other personal gear. 60 minutes.

DVD: $25.00 **ISBN: 1-57188-335-5**
UPC: 0-81127-00169-9

COLOR GUIDE TO STEELHEAD DRIFT FISHING
Bill Herzog

Each year nearly 1,000,000 steelhead are hooked in North America and the great majority of these fish are hooked using drift fishing techniques. This lavishly illustrated, all-color guide is the "bible" if you want to get in on the action. Written by one of America's greatest drift fishermen, you will learn the techniques that can guarantee your entry into the 10% of the anglers who hook 90% of the steelhead. This is a heavy-duty graduate course! 8 1/2 x 11 inches, 80 pages.

SB: $19.95 **ISBN: 1-878175-59-9**
UPC: 0-66066-00150-4

SPOON FISHING FOR STEELHEAD
Bill Herzog

One of the most effective ways to hook steelhead (and salmon) is with a spoon. Bill Herzog covers spoon fishing techniques for the full year, going into finishes, sizes, weights, shapes, water temperature differences, winter and summer fish differences, commercial and custom spoons, spoon parts suppliers, and reading water. Scores of color photos enhance the book, along with many line drawings, graphs and illustrations. 8 1/2 x 11 inches, 64 pages.

SB: $14.95 **ISBN: 1-878175-30-0**
UPC: 0-66066-00119-1

STEELHEAD & SALMON DRIFT-FISHING SECRETS
Timothy Kusherets

This comprehensive book goes way beyond the basics of drift-fishing techniques to include marine biology, ichthyology, meteorology, and physics as they apply to fish and fishing.

Kusherets covers: species identification and anatomy; gear; set-ups; reading water; different drifting styles and techniques; understanding fish; spotting fish; troubleshooting; using the Internet; filleting your catch; extensive glossary; and more. The unique book will bring more fish to your line. 6 x 9 inches, 96 pages.

SB: $16.95 **ISBN: 1-57188-300-2**
UPC: 0-81127-00134-7

FLOAT FISHING FOR STEELHEAD TECHNIQUES & TACKLE
Dave Vedder

"Float fishing for winter or summer steelhead is terribly productive. It is uncomplicated and the hook-set is almost always effective as opposed to drift fishing. Float fishing is the easiest (no snags), most effective way to hook steelhead. Vedder's all-color book explains all the methodology and tackle choices. This is the wave of the future."

—Frank W. Amato 5 1/2 x 8 1/2 inches, 64 pages.

SB: $15.95 **ISBN: 1-57188-039-9**
UPC: 0-66066-00230-3

SUMMER STEELHEAD FISHING TECHNIQUES
Scott Haugen

Scott Haugen is quickly becoming known for his fact-filled, full-color fishing books. This time Haugen explores summer steelhead, including: understanding summer steelhead; reading water; bank, drift, and sight fishing; jigs, plugs, lures, dragging flies, and bait; fishing high, turbid waters; tying your own leaders; egg cures; gathering bait; do-it-yourself sinkers; hatchery and recycling programs; mounting your catch; cleaning and preparation; smoking your catch; and more. 6 x 9 inches, 135 pages.

SB: $15.95 **ISBN: 1-57188-295-2**
UPC: 0-81127-00125-5

EGG CURES: Proven Recipes & Techniques
Scott Haugen

Of all the natural baits, many consider eggs to be the best. Before this book, you'd have an easier time getting the secret recipe for Coca-Cola than getting a fisherman to part with his personal egg cure. But now, Scott Haugen has done it for you, he went to the experts—fishermen and fishing guides—to get their favorite egg cures and fishing techniques, plus their secret tricks and tips. The result is this book. These 28 recipes come from anglers who catch fish—read this book and you will too. Guaranteed! 5 1/2 x 8 1/2 inches, 90 pages.

SB: $15.00 **ISBN: 1-57188-238-3**
UPC: 0-66066-00492-5

SPINNER FISHING FOR STEELHEAD, SALMON AND TROUT
Jed Davis

The "bible" for spinner fishing and the most in-depth, non-fly-fishing book ever written about steelhead and their habits. Information on how to make spinners is complete, including how to assemble, obtain parts, even how to silver plate. The fishing techniques, lure, line color and size selection, and reading fish-holding water sections are excellent. 8 1/2 x 11 inches, 97 pages.

SB: $19.95 **ISBN: 0-936608-40-4**
UPC: 0-66066-00056-9

STEELHEAD FISHING ESSENTIALS - BOOK/DVD SET
By Marc Davis

Marc Davis has been pursuing steelhead for several decades. He shares his years of experience, on the page and also in person with the exciting 100-minute DVD that puts Davis's words into action. Davis, and other expert steelheaders, discuss equipment, tackle, baits, reading water, techniques from the bank or boat, scents, casting, conservation, and more. Dramatic underwater footage and adrenaline-pumping fights on the DVD give action—and credibility—to Davis's steelheading expertise. All color, 6 x 9 inches, 165 pages.

SB w/DVD: $29.95
ISBN-13: 978-1-57188-450-3
UPC: 0-81127-00286-3

SIDE-DRIFTING FOR STEELHEAD
Nick Amato, Mike Perusse and Travis Price

Side-drifting for steelhead and salmon is becoming one of the most popular angling methods used on the West Coast. This instructional video will show you how to quickly master the techniques necessary to side-drift effectively from a drift boat, jet boat or the bank. Subjects covered include: Boat handling and positioning, reading water, terminal tackle, rods and reels, sinker types, bait and boating etiquette. Nick and Mike get numerous steelhead on film—from strike to release. Whether you are an expert or novice side-drifter this DVD will get you revved up to get on the water! 60 minutes.

DVD: $25.00 **ISBN: 1-57188-353-3**
UPC: 0-81127-00187-3

FLOAT FISHING FOR STEELHEAD
with Nick, Rob, and Matt

Float-fishing for steelhead is very productive. It's the easiest and most effective way to hook steelhead. Nick Amato, Rob Crandall, and Canadian float-fishing expert Matt Guiguet, share the secrets for successful float-fishing. They cover: Rigging floats, jigs, and gear; fishing techniques and tips; equipment; reading water; and more. If you are looking to hook more steelhead, look no further. 60 minutes.

DVD: $25.00 **ISBN: 1-57188-331-2**
UPC: 0-81127-00168-2

VIDEO: $25.00 **ISBN: 1-57188-249-9**
UPC: 0-66066-00502-1

STEELHEAD FLOAT FISHING
Jim Butler

Take a look down any stream in the Great Lakes during the fall or spring steelhead season and one thing is clear—the majority of anglers have turned to float fishing to help them catch more steelhead. Float fishing, over all other methods and presentations, is responsible for more hooked steelhead throughout the Great Lakes tributaries than any other fishing method. In this book, Jim shares all that you need to know, including: the history, strategies and behaviors of steelhead; reading water; float-fishing techniques; natural and artificial baits; fall, winter, and spring steelhead; float reels and how to cast them; building balsa floats; the future of the fishery; and so much more. If you want to catch more steelhead, this book will show you how. 8 1/2 x 11 inches, 80 pages.

SB: $19.95 **ISBN: 1-57188-322-3**
UPC: 0-81127-00156-9

Ask for these books at your local fishing or book store, or order from:
Frank Amato Publications, Inc. ■ P.O. Box 82112 ■ Portland, Oregon 97282
1-800-541-9498 (8 to 5 P.S.T.) ■ or www.amatobooks.com